WRITER-FILES

General Editor: Simon Trussler

Associate Editor: Malcolm Page

File on
PIRANDELLO

Compiled by Susan Bassnett

Methuen Drama

A Methuen Drama Book
First published in 1989 as a paperback original
by Methuen Drama, Michelin House,
81 Fulham Road, London SW3 6RB,
and HEB Inc., 70 Court Street, Portsmouth,
New Hampshire 03801, USA

Typeset in 9/10 Times by
L. Anderson Typesetting,
Woodchurch, Kent TN26 3TB

Printed in Great Britain by
Cox and Wyman Ltd., Reading

ISBN 0-413-17340-2

British Library Cataloguing in Publication Data
is available from the British Library

Contents

The theatre is, by its nature, an ephemeral art: yet it is a daunt-
ing task to track down the newspaper reviews, or contemporary statements from the writer or his director, which are often
all that remain to help us recreate some sense of what a particular production was like. This series is therefore intended to
make readily available a selection of the comments that the
critics made about the plays of leading modern dramatists at
the time of their production — and to trace, too, the course of
each writer's own views about his work and his world.

In addition to combining a uniquely convenient source of
such elusive *documentation*, the 'Writer-Files' series also
assembles the *information* necessary for readers to pursue
further their interest in a particular writer or work. Variations
in quantity between one writer's output and another's,
differences in temperament which make some readier than
others to talk about their work, and the variety of critical
response, all mean that the presentation and balance of
material shifts between one volume and another: but we have
tried to arrive at a format for the series which will nevertheless
enable users of one volume readily to find their way around
any other.

Section 1, 'A Brief Chronology', provides a quick conspec-
tive overview of each playwright's life and career. *Section 2*
deals with the plays themselves, arranged chronologically in
the order of their composition: information on first performances, major revivals, and publication is followed by a
brief synopsis (for quick reference set in slightly larger, italic
type), then by a representative selection of the critical
response, and of the dramatist's own comments on the play
and its theme.

Section 3 offers concise guidance to each writer's work in
non-dramatic forms, while *Section 4*, 'The Writer on His
Work', brings together comments from the playwright himself
on more general matters of construction, opinion, and artistic
development. Finally, *Section 5* provides a bibliographical
guide to other primary and secondary sources of further reading, among which full details will be found of works cited
elsewhere under short titles, and of collected editions of the
plays — but not of individual titles, particulars of which will
be found with the other factual data in Section 2.

The 'Writer-Files' hope by striking this kind of balance
between information and a wide range of opinion to offer
'companions' to the study of major playwrights in the modern
repertoire — not in that dangerous pre-digested fashion which

General Editor's Introduction

can too readily quench the desire to read the plays themselves, nor so prescriptively as to allow any single line of approach to predominate, but rather to encourage readers to form their own judgements of the plays in a wide-ranging context.

Luigi Pirandello today seems both distinctly old-fashioned and strikingly modern: old-fashioned for the framework of domestic naturalism within which he so often seems to entrap a dramatic action — before (often) exploding its boundaries — and (more specifically) for the streak of misogyny which is liable to break through from the personality into the plays. Yet in his constant questioning of the nature of truth and assertion of the impossibility of verification he both anticipated Pinter, and, as one of the reviewers of *Henry IV* (quoted on page 49 of this volume) points out, came close in his perception of madness to the views of R. D. Laing. In more strictly theatrical terms, Pirandello recognized and portrayed long before Alan Ayckbourn the broad spectrum from comedy to tragedy along which may be plotted the private angsts of adultery and the love-hatred which frays so many sexual and family ties.

Those six characters for ever eponymously in search of their author enjoy the odd distinction of having entered into the common stock of contemporary allusions far more pervasively than they have into the international dramatic repertoire. For, with the other exceptions of *Henry IV* and *The Rules of the Game*, Pirandello's writing remains largely neglected outside his own country. The balance of this volume falls more heavily, therefore, than in many others of this series upon the communication simply of what the plays are about. But reviews of English-language productions often less helpfully insist on the need to explicate *meaning*, as if this were always to be found somewhere enkernelled within Pirandello's multi-layered perceptions. One may or may not admire what the reviewer quoted on page 45 calls the 'practical cunning whereby he has made metaphysics actable', yet, as the compiler of the present volume has elsewhere pointed out, Pirandello's work, consummately theatrical though it usually is (and deliciously *funny* though it can less expectedly be), is based on the recognition of a paradox — that while any art 'is a kind of death, since it freezes and fixes the unfixable', the creation of just such 'illusory' structures to make life supportable is 'the only way to endow existence with any meaning'.

Pirandello collected his plays as *Naked Masks* — but not from any assumption that 'truth' lay hidden beneath. His art at its best captures the awful yet sometimes comic collisions which occur when the mask is ripped away, only to reveal ... another mask. As Martin Esslin has suggested, Pirandello is the dramatist of relativity, whose Einsteinian universe spins in his own bedroom and his own back-yard.

Simon Trussler

1867 28 June, born in Girgenti, Sicily, son of Stefano Pirandello, wealthy sulphur mine contractor and Caterina Ricci Gramitto. Childhood spent in Girgenti, in farmhouse known as Il caos (Chaos).

1887 Goes to Rome to study law.

1888-95 Studies philology at University of Bonn. Love relationship with Jenny Schulz Lander.

1889 First collection of poems published in Sicily, entitled *Mal Giocondo (Unhappy Joy)*.

1891 Settled definitively in Rome as a 'man of letters'. Second collection of poems, *Pasqua di Gea (Gea's Easter)*, published in Milan.

1894 First collection of short stories, *Amori senza amore (Loveless Loves)* published in Milan. Marries Antonietta Portulano, daughter of his father's business partner.

1895 Third collection of poems, *Elegie renane (Rhine Elegies)* published in Rome. Birth of his son, Stefano.

1896 Translates Goethe's *Roman Elegies*, published in Leghorn.

1897 Birth of his daughter, Lietta. Takes up teaching post at Magistero in Rome (teacher training college) where he remained until 1922.

1899 Birth of his third and last child, Fausto. Antonietta has her first nervous breakdown.

1901 His first novel, *L'esclusa (The Outcast)*, originally written in 1893, is serialized in *La Tribuna* (eventually published as a book in 1908).

1902 Second novel, *Il turno (The Shift)*, published in Catania. Two collections of short stories published, *Beffe della morte e della vita (Jokes about Life and Death)* and *Quand' ero matto (When I Was Mad)*.

1903 Floods in sulphur mine result in loss of Stefano

Pirandello's capital together with Antonietta's money. Antonietta suffers mental collapse, resulting in temporary psychosomatic paralysis.

1904 Publication of *Il fu Mattia Pascal (He Was Mattia Pascal)*, the novel which brought him major literary success in Italy. Collection of stories published, entitled *Bianche e nere (Black and White)*.

1906 Collection of stories published, entitled *Erma bifronte (Two-faced Erma)*.

1908 Third novel published, *I vecchi e i giovani (The Old and the Young)*. Novel consciously explores Pirandello's political attitudes and beliefs, revealing his inclination towards rightist views. *L'umorismo (Essay on Humour)* published — one of Pirandello's most crucial essays, in which he outlines his philosophy of humour.

1910 Two one-act plays, *Lumíe di Sicilia (Sicilian Limes)* and *La morsa (The Bit*, written *c.* 1892), presented at Teatro Metastasio, Rome, directed by Nino Martoglio (1870-1921). This production marks the start of a close collaboration with Martoglio. For the next six years Pirandello took up the cause of promoting a Sicilian dialect theatre, working with Martoglio and writing for the Sicilian actor Angelo Musco (1872-1937). Further collection of short stories, *La vita nuda (Naked Life)*, published.

1911 Fourth novel published, *Suo marito (Her Husband)*.

1912 Collection of poems published, *Fuori di chiave (Out of Key)*, and further collection of short stories, *Terzetti*.

1915 Italy declares war on Austria. Pirandello's sons are called up.

1916 Further collections of short stories published: *La trappola (The Trap)* and *Erba del nostro orto (Grass from our Garden)*. First performances of *Liolà* at Teatro Argentina, Rome, and *Pensaci, Giacomino (Think It Over, Giacomino)* at Teatro Nazionale, Rome. Both in Sicilian dialect, these were to be two of his most popular works. Novel published in serial form, entitled *Si gira (Shoot)*.

1917 First performances of *Il beretto a sonagli (Cap and Bells)* and *La giara (The Jar)*, both in Sicilian dialect, at Teatro Nazionale, Rome. Acutely depressed by news of son Stefano's imprisonment and Antonietta's decline into madness, Pirandello begins to write increasingly for Italian theatre, moving away from earlier commitment to dialect theatre. First performance of his major three-act play in Italian, *Così è (se vi pare) (Right You Are, If You Think So)*, at Teatro Olimpia, Milan.

1918 Antonietta committed to a mental hospital, where she remained for another thirty years. In 1924, in reply to a journalist interested in the recurring theme of madness in Pirandello's theatre, Pirandello comments that seeing 'life transposed in the mind of my poor companion, enabled me later to convey the psychology of the alienated in my creative writing'. Further collection of short stories published, *Un cavallo nella luna (A Horse in the Moon)*. Two further plays performed, *Ma non è una cosa seria (But It's Not Serious)* at Teatro Rossini, Leghorn, and *Il giuoco delle parti (The Rules of the Game)* at Teatro Quirino, Rome.

1919 Collaborates with Martoglio in directing Teatro Mediterraneo Company at Teatro Argentina, Rome, and obtains first-hand experience of live theatre. Translates Euripides' *Cyclops* into Sicilian for this company. Two collections of short stories published: *Il carnevale dei morti (The Carnival of the Dead)* and *Berecche e la guerra (Berecche and the War)*, his most explicit account of the miseries he had experienced during the First World War. Three further plays performed: *L'innesto (The Grafting)* at Teatro Manzoni, Milan, *La patente (By Judgement of Court)* at Teatro Olimpia, Milan, and *L'uomo, la bestia e la virtù (Man, Beast and Virtue)* at Teatro Olimpia, Milan.

1920 Three more plays: *Tutto per bene (All for the Best)* at Teatro Quirino, Rome, *Come prima, meglio di prima (As Before, Better than Before)* at Teatro Goldoni, Venice, and *La Signora Morli, una e due (The Two Signora Morlis)* at Teatro Argentina, Rome.

1921 10 May, first performance of *Sei personaggi in cerca d'autore (Six Characters in Search of an Author)* at Teatro Argentina, Rome. The first night ends in a riot, with fighting in the streets, but by September, when revived at Teatro Manzoni, Milan, public response is ecstatic. Between 1922 and 1927 there were performances of the play throughout Europe, in the US, in Argentina and in Japan. After Pitöeff's 1923 production and Reinhardt's 1924 production, the play was substantially rewritten in the light of insights produced in performances.

1922 24 February, first performance of *Enrico IV (Henry IV)* at Teatro Manzoni, Milan. Written especially for the actor Ruggero Ruggeri, this play has been translated more frequently into English than any other of Pirandello's works, and has often been described as comparable to a

Shakespearean tragedy. First performances of *Vestire gli ignudi (To Clothe the Naked)* at Teatro Quirino, Rome. Pirandello had become an international celebrity overnight and for the remainder of his life was to travel widely outside Italy. 28 October, Mussolini and his Blackshirts march on Rome.

1923 First performance of *L'uomo dal fiore in bocca (The Man with the Flower in his Mouth)* at Teatro Degli Indipendenti, Rome. *La vita che ti diedi (The Life I Gave You)* at Teatro Quirino, Rome. This play had been written for Eleonora Duse, but she declined to perform it for unspecified reasons.

1924 10 June, murder of Giacomo Matteotti, Socialist MP, by Mussolini's Blackshirts. 19 September, Pirandello gives a copy of his letter to Mussolini asking to join the Fascist Party to the fascist newspaper *L'Impero*. Debate as to the full extent of Pirandello's commitment to fascism begins as a result of this gesture and is still going on today. Together with a group of colleagues, Pirandello decides to found an Italian Arts Theatre. He obtains government assistance for the project and takes over the Teatro Odescalchi in Rome as a base for his company. On 22 May at the Teatro dei Filodrammatici, Milan, *Ciascuno a suo modo (Each in His Own Way)* is first performed. He meets Marta Abba, the actress for whom most of his later plays were written. He is now 57 years old.

1925 Last novel published, entitled *Uno, nessuno e centomila (One, No-one and a Hundred Thousand)*. 4 April, Arts Theatre opens with a production of Pirandello's first attempt at mass theatre, *La Sagra del Signore della nave (The Tale of Our Lord of the Ship)* and Alfred Dunsany's *The Gods of the Mountain*. Pirandello was now not only writing plays but actively involved in theatre management and directing. His company toured extensively — in Italy, Europe, North and South America — until the collapse of the Teatro d'Arte for financial reasons in 1928.

1926 *Diana e la Tuda (Diana and Tuda)*, written for Marta Abba, premieres in Hans Feist's German version at the Schauspielhaus, Zurich, on 20 November. The play was not performed in Italian until January 1927, and during the next few years it was to become a frequent pattern for Pirandello's plays to open outside Italy.

1927 28 April, first performance of *L'amica delle mogli (The Wives' Friend)* at Teatro Argentina, Rome.

1928   Decides to leave Italy following collapse of Arts Theatre project and decline in popularity. Moves to Germany in the hope of beginning a new phase of his career by working in cinema. First performance of *La nuova colonia (The New Colony)* at Teatro Argentina, Rome. He described this play as a 'myth' and turned increasingly to writing heavily symbolic plays with huge casts and complex staging.

1929   First performance of another mythical play, *Lazzaro (Lazarus)*, entitled *Though One Rose*, at Theatre Royal, Huddersfield, in English version by C. K. Scott-Moncrieff.

1930   First performance of *Questa sera si recita a soggeto (Tonight We Improvise)*, entitled *Heute Abend wird aus dem Stegreif Gespielt*, in German version by Harry Kahn at Koenigsberg. The play was a failure and Pirandello was so embittered by its reception that he left Germany in disgust. Together with *Six Characters* and *Each in His Own Way*, this play completes the trilogy of 'theatre-in-the-theatre' plays.

1932   First performance of *Trovarsi (Finding Oneself)* at the Teatro dei Fiorentini, Naples.

1933   First performance of bitterly autobiographical fable *Quando si è qualcuno (When One is Somebody)*, Teatro Odeon, Buenos Aires.

1934   Awarded the Nobel Prize for literature. First performance of *Non si sa come (You Don't Know How)*, the last work Pirandello finished before his death.

1936   10 December, died in Rome. His last wishes are simple: *Burn me. And as soon as my body has been burnt the ashes must be thrown to the winds, for I want nothing, not even my ashes, to remain. But if this cannot be done the funeral urn must be taken to Sicily and walled into some rough stone near Agrigento, where I was born.* This last request was ignored.

1937   Posthumous performance of his major work, *I giganti della montagna (The Mountain Giants)*, in Boboli Gardens, Florence. Last unfinished play (third act unwritten) is a parable about processes of creating theatre and power of social forces in opposition to art on an enormous scale. It has rarely been revived, most significantly by Giorgio Strehler in 1967 in a production that heralded a reappraisal of Pirandello, long ignored as a fascist writer, in changing Italian social context.

The Vice (La morsa)

One-act play for four actors.

First production: Teatro Metastasio, Rome, 9 Dec. 1910
(Teatro Minimo Company, dir. Nino Martoglio).

First published: as a short story entitled 'L'epilogo', in *Ariel*
(Rome), 20 March 1898; as a play, in *Noi e il Mondo,*
1 March 1914.

Translations: Elizabeth Abbot, in Arthur Livingston, ed.,
Pirandello's One-Act Plays (New York, Dutton, 1928);
William Murray, *Pirandello's One-Act Plays* (New York,
Doubleday, 1964).

First British production: Garden Theatre, London, 1 July
1928.

---

*The play takes up the familiar Pirandellian theme of
adulterous passion. Andrea and Antonio have been
away together on business, but Antonio suspects that
Andrea saw him kissing Giulia before they left. The
action begins with Antonio confiding this suspicion to
Giulia. The lovers become increasingly agitated as they
speculate over what Andrea might actually know about
their relationship and become more convinced that they
have been found out. Antonio leaves as Andrea returns
home. Andrea baits a trap for his wife and finally
accuses her outright. Giulia at first denies the charge,
but then is caught in what Andrea terms 'the vice' that
he steadily tightens around her, the vice of using the
story of another woman's adultery to force his wife to
expose herself. Giulia breaks down and confesses.
Andrea furiously calls her a whore and orders her out
of the house. She begs to be allowed to see her children
once more before she goes, but Andrea refuses. As she
looks out of the window to catch a glimpse of them,
Andrea points out the figure of Antonio coming back to
the house. Giulia runs into the next room and shoots
herself. As Antonio comes in, Andrea turns and shouts
the word 'murderer' at him, and the curtain falls.*

Sicilian Limes (Lumìe di Sicilia)

One-act play for five actors.

First production: Teatro Metastasio, Rome, 9 Dec. 1910 (Teatro Minimo Company, dir. Nino Martoglio).

First published: as a short story, in *Il Marzocco*, 20 and 27 May 1900; as a play, in *Nuova antologia*, 16 March 1911.

Revivals: in Sicilian dialect, Teatro Pacini, Catania, 7 July 1915 (Angelo Musco's Company); Teatro Manzoni, Milan, 7 Feb. 1937 (Sica-Rissone-Melnati Company, with Vittorio de Sica as Micuccio).

First British production: BBC Third Programme, 9 July 1955 (trans. Robert Rietti).

Translations: Isaac Goldberg, in John Liuce, *Plays of the Italian Theatre* (1921); Elizabeth Abbot, in Arthur Livingston, ed., *Pirandello's One-Act Plays* (New York: Dutton, 1928); William Murray, *Pirandello's One-Act Plays* (New York: Doubleday, 1964).

Micuccio, a poor Sicilian villager, arrives at the home of Sina Maurus, a famous singer, who now lives somewhere in the wealthy North of Italy. Ferdinando and Dorina, two of Sina's servants, are sneeringly amused by Micuccio's account of his early relationship with Sina when she was an unknown peasant girl. He has come to repay an old debt and to see the woman he launched on her singing career and who had once promised to marry him. The sniggering servants make fun of the naive Micuccio, who is unaware of the social distance that now separates him from Sina. Marta, Sina's mother, arrives, and a party for Sina begins in the next room to which Micuccio is not invited. Marta tries to hide her embarrassment by offering him food and chatting about old times in the village, but the raucous noise of the party keeps disturbing them and Micuccio begins to feel more and more out of place. Finally, he realizes that Sina's lifestyle has changed out of all recognition and that she is now a woman of the world, and no longer the innocent girl he believes he has loved. When Sina finally runs in, wearing a low-cut evening dress, Micuccio accuses her of being unworthy of him. He throws the bag of limes from the village that he has brought as a gift for her onto the table, ordering her not to touch them with her soiled hands. In a parting gesture, he stuffs

*the money he owes her down the front of her dress and rushes
out of her life forever.*

Sicilian Limes is an exquisite dialogue piece, packed with humour and
painful human feeling.

Anonymous review in *Il Messagero*, 11 Dec. 1910

Last night I went to the Teatro Morgana to see a performance of *Sicilian
Limes*, which has been a great success thanks to the marvellous acting of
(Angelo) Musco.

What a pity that Zia Marta was such an abomination. But, I must say
it again, the play has been a complete success.

Luigi Pirandello to his son, Stefano, 25 Feb. 1916

The Doctor's Duty (Il dovere del medico)

One-act play with parts for seven actors.
First production: Sala Umberto I, Rome, 20 June 1913 (Teatro per Tutti
Company, dir. Lucio d'Ambra and Achille Vitti).
First published: as a short story, in the collection *La vita nuda* (Rome:
Treves, 1910); as a play, in *Noi e il mondo*, Jan. 1912.
Translations: Blanche Valentine Mitchell, in Arthur Livingston, ed.,
Pirandello's One-Act Plays (New York: Dutton, 1928); William
Murray, *Pirandello's One-Act Plays* (New York: Doubleday, 1964).

*Before the action begins, Tommaso has been found in bed with
the wife of Neri, the assistant district attorney. In the ensuing
struggle, Tommaso has killed Neri, the wife has killed herself,
and Tommaso has been seriously injured. The play opens with
Signora Reis, Tommaso's mother-in-law, and Anna, his wife,
talking about what has happened. Anna wants her husband to
recover, but Signora Reis wants the policeman waiting in the
house to take him to gaol. Lecci, the local doctor, and Cimetta, a
lawyer, come to confront Tommaso and prepare him for his
eventual arrest on murder charges, but when Tommaso appears
the tables are turned. Tommaso accuses Dr. Lecci of the crime of
having saved him. He argues that after killing Neri he had tried*

to do the honourable thing of turning the gun on himself and has since tried several times to tear off his bandages and bleed to death. Lecci's duty, according to Tommaso, was not to save his life but to let him die with honour. At the conclusion of this exchange, Tommaso tears off his bandages again, but this time Dr. Lecci fulfils that other duty and the curtain falls as he stands by, refusing to cross the room and help the dying man.

Other People's Reason (La ragione degli altri)

Play in three acts.
First production: under the title *Se non così . . .*, Teatro Manzoni, Milan, 19 April 1915 (Milan Repertory Company, dir. Marco Praga).
Revivals: Teatro Valle, Rome, 16 Dec. 1919 (Luisa Carini Company); Teatro Eliseo, Rome, 20 Feb. 1942 (dir. Ermete Zacconi); Teatro della Cometa, Rome, 24 Apr. 1961 (dir. Diego Fabbri).
First published: in *Nuova antologia*, Rome, Jan. 1916; also in *Maschere nude*, Vol. IV (Milan: Treves, 1921).

Pirandello's first three-act play opens with Livia Arciani arriving unexpectedly at her husband Leonardo's office. Leonardo is a political journalist, and from his colleague De Alis's reception of Livia it is obvious that the marriage has been in difficulties for some time. Livia is a wealthy woman and her father, Guglielmo Groa, is a highly influential man. Despite their difficulties, Livia and Leonardo have stayed together, and there are strong hints that this has been out of convenience. When Livia leaves, Elena Orgera, Leonardo's mistress, comes to see him to ask for more money. The relationship between the two of them is obviously problematic, and when Guglielmo arrives to demand that Leonardo give up Elena and return to his wife, it becomes clear that this is also what Elena and Leonardo would prefer. But Elena has a daughter by Leonardo and he refuses to give up the child. Faced with the dilemma of her erring husband who wants to return to her, Livia gives him an ultimatum: he must choose between her and his daughter. Then she goes to see Elena, and the last act consists of the confrontation between the two women. Elena tells Livia that the love between her and

Leonardo is over, and he can return home with her blessing. But Livia refuses to take him back without his daughter, arguing that now he is not only a husband or lover but also a father. She gives Elena the choice of either staying in a loveless relationship with Leonardo or giving up her daughter to be brought up as the child of her father and the wealthy Livia. Elena finally concedes, and the play ends with Leonardo taking the child away and Elena, alone, sitting in a chair clutching the little girl's bonnet and sobbing in despair.

We must not forget that this play is by Luigi Pirandello, one of our most original writers and one of the most perceptive, lively creators of characters. And although it is a dismal mistake, there are some signs of the great intellect behind it. There are refined touches of dialogue, seriousness and the most interesting intentions. But it is hard to perceive them because the whole piece lacks shape as a work of theatre.

Renato Simoni, *Il Corriere della Sera*, 20 Apr. 1915

I am sorry to have to tell you that you do not create a very good impression in this play. Possibly no leading actress with an ounce of self-respect would confess to being willing to undertake a part such as the one you play in this work. . . .

Are you the main character or not? It does not matter, dear lady. It may well be true that everything that happens in all three acts only happens because of the way you think and feel. . . . But what is also true, dear lady, is what I told you in the beginning: that you do not create a very good impression in this play. So stay here, on the written page.

On the stages of today, being as you are, you cannot make much headway, I do assure you. You simply do not possess, dear lady, that which might be termed in the jargon of the theatre, the show-stopping moment.

Luigi Pirandello, letter to the main character, Signora Livia Arciani, included as Preface to the published edition

Think It Over, Giacomino
(Pensaci, Giacomino)

First production: Teatro Nazionale, Rome, 10 July 1916 (Angelo

Musco's Company, dir. Angelo Musco), in repertoire until 1936.
Revivals: from 1920-1936, in repertoire of Mediterranean Company
(dir. Giovanni Grasso); from 1932-1948, in repertoire of various
companies directed by Sergio Tofano; from 1950-1960, in repertoire
of Compagnia del Teatro di Sicilia (dir. Michele Abruzzo); Teatro
Pirandello, Rome, 1 Dec. 1955 (dir. Luigi Almirante); Teatro
dell'Arte al Parco di Milano, Feb. 1968 (dir. Sergio Bargone); Teatro
Eliseo, Rome, Mar. 1981 (dir. Nello Rossati; with Salvo Randone as
Professor Toti).
First British production: Rudolf Steiner Theatre, London, 25 Oct. 1953
(trans. Victor Rietti).
Film version: 1936 (dir. Gennaro Righelli; with Angelo Musco).
First published: Noi e il mondo, Rome, 1 Apr.-1 June 1917; also in
Maschere nude, Vol. I (Milan: Treves, 1918).
Translation: Victor Rietti (unpublished), 1953.

---

*Agostino Toti, an old schoolmaster with an overwhelming love
for humanity, has married Lillina, a young girl thrown out of the
house of her parents when they discover that she is pregnant.
Toti has made her his wife and given her the comfortable house
he has inherited, and has also agreed to be husband in name
only so that Lillina can continue to meet her lover, Giacomino
Delisi, every day. They have a child, Nini, whom Toti adores, and
Toti has even found Giacomino a job in the local bank so that
the lovers can live as happily as possible. But the forces of
respectability, as personified in Lillina's parents, Rosaria,
Giacomino's fanatically religious sister, the headmaster of Toti's
school and Padre Landolina (one of Pirandello's strongest anti-
clerical portraits), unite to try and plot an end to what they
perceive as a scandal. Giacomino stops coming to Toti's house
to see Lillina and his son, and when Toti learns that pressure
has been brought to bear on him, he confronts Giacomino who
has gone into hiding at his sister's house, and is considering
marriage to a respectable young woman. Toti convinces
Giacomino that if he goes ahead with the marriage he will
destroy the happiness of both Lillina and little Nini. By the end
of the play Toti has become the champion of the individual's
right to live according to his own laws. He persuades
Giacomino to walk out of Rosaria's house, ignoring the vocifer-
ous appeals of the respectable characters, taking his little boy*

with him, to return to the way of life that he had previously enjoyed.

I promised Musco I'd make him a three-act play out of my story, *Pensaci, Giacomino,* and I've already done the basic shaping. I hope it will work. Musco comes back to the National in May and I hope to have the play ready by May.

Luigi Pirandello to Stefano Pirandello, 25 Feb. 1916

I have to tell you something that will make you very happy. Last night Musco performed my play, *Pensaci, Giacomino,* at the National, and it was a triumph. At the end of the third act the audience jumped up to a man and called me out in front of the curtain six times, though I did not appear. The first act had four curtain calls and the second act had two; twelve curtain calls in all. But it was a great victory because the piece is very daring, and the audience was not inclined to applaud. The whole play was listened to with such rapt attention that one almost felt frightened by it. Musco was magnificent.

Luigi Pirandello to Stefano Pirandello, 10 July 1916

Liolà

First production: in Sicilian dialect, Teatro Argentina, Rome,
4 Nov. 1916 (Angelo Musco's Company); in Italian language, Teatro Orfeo, Rome, 12 Nov. 1929 (dir. Ignazio Mascalchi).
Revivals: following the 1937 publication of the revised Italian-language version: Teatro Nuovo, Milan, 8 June 1942 (Tofano-Rissone-De Sica Company); Teatro Quirino, Rome, 30 Oct. 1961 (dir. Vittorio de Sica); Teatro Circo, Rome, 23 Oct. 1968 (dir. Giorgio Prosperi).
First published: Rome: Formiggini, 1917 (Sicilian text with Italian translation on facing pages); in *Maschere nude,* Vol. XXIV, second edition (Florence: Bemporad, 1928).
Translation: Eric Bentley and G. Guerrieri, in Eric Bentley, *Naked Masks* (New York: Dutton, 1952).
First British production: Civic Theatre, Leeds, 3 Sept. 1956 (trans. and dir. Frederick May).

Liolà is a peasant who loves women, and whenever his various lovers give birth to children, he takes them under his protection and gives them to his mother, Zia Ninfa, to bring up. He first appears accompanied by three of his children, whom he describes as three parts of himself. In contrast to his fecundity is Zio Simone, a wealthy old man who has married Mita, the girl Liolà once loved. Mita's aged husband not only maltreats her, but in four years of marriage he has been unable to make her pregnant. Meanwhile, Tuzza, a village girl who has turned down Liolà's offer of marriage, declares that she is pregnant and that the father is Zio Simone. The old man is delighted, but in fact the child is Liolà's and the unscrupulous Tuzza and her mother have only been trying to convince Zio Simone that he is the father in hope that he will disinherit the unfortunate Mita in Tuzza's favour. Liolà offers to help Mita by fathering a child for her, and after some persuasion Mita agrees. In Act Two she breaks the news to Zio Simone that he is about to become a father of a legitimate heir. Tuzza is outwitted by this move and tries to take revenge on Liolà by stabbing him, but only succeeds in wounding him. The play ends with Liolà surrounded by his children, promising Tuzza that he will care for her child also.

In this play there are touches of bitter, melancholy spite, and anger glitters through the smile against women in general, who come off worst in *Liolà*. But one should not be surprised at this. A good half of the theatre of all times is anti-feminist. Modern theatre is slightly less so, but the ancient theatre always was.

Renato Simoni, *Il Corriere della Sera*, Milan, 14 Jan. 1917

In reconsidering Pirandello today, fifteen years after his death (1951), the first play to read is *Liolà*. It loses more than other plays in translation, but perhaps enough of the original comes through to remove the anti-Pirandello prejudice. It is a play that lives by an evident loveliness. . . . *Liolà* is a play for the 1950s. Amid the spurious apocalyptics of the few and the genuine hysteria of the many — so far the only spiritual manifestations of the atomic age — anything that recalls us to sanity is welcome. Pirandello's tidings of great joy are the best 'message' any theatrical manager of today could find.

Eric Bentley, '*Liolà* and Other Plays',
reprinted in *The Pirandello Commentaries* (1986)

Since the advent of feminist criticism, it has become impossible not to read *Liolà* as a tasteless example of reactionary male chauvinism. . . . What Pirandello seems to have done is create a work in which he 'tried to rival the ancient spirit of the sixteenth century'. That he failed to do so is an indication of the essential flaw in his apolitical stance, for in the make-believe Sicilian village of *Liolà*, compromise and deceit ultimately triumph. Life, says Liolà, is enjoyment and love and fecundity, and one feels that Pirandello, in the world of the Great War, living with his paranoid wife, must have longed to believe such an idea. But ultimately Liolà's ways are destructive — he degrades women, forces his mother to bring up his children, condemns those children to a motherless existence and incites others to lie and deceive. Man is a loving island, Liolà proclaims, but such a notion is as illusory as the world of the play.

Susan Bassnett-McGuire, *Luigi Pirandello* (1983)

Right You Are (If You Think So)
(Cosí é, se vi pare)

First production: Teatro Olimpico, Milan, 18 June 1917 (Virgilio Talli's Company).

Revivals: Teatro Argentina, Rome, Mar. 1927 (Teatro d'Arte Company, dir. Luigi Pirandello; with Marta Abba and Lamberto Picasso); Teatro Argentina, Rome, 21 Jan. 1939 (Spettacoli Errepi Company, with Ruggero Ruggeri and Irma Gramatica); Teatro Quirino, Rome, 5 Feb. 1965 (Rina Morelli and Paolo Stoppa Company, dir. Mario Ferrero); Teatro Duse, Bologna, May 1983 (dir. Giancarlo Sepe; with Lilla Brignone).

First British production: as *And That's the Truth!*, Lyric Theatre, Hammersmith, 17 Sept. 1925 (trans. Arthur Livingston; dir. Nigel Playfair).

First US production: 44th Street Theatre, New York, Jan. 1924 (trans. Arthur Livingston).

First published: Nuova antologia, Rome, 1-16 Jan. 1918; also in *Maschere nude*, Vol. I (Milan, Treves, 1918).

Translations: Arthur Livingston, *Three Plays* (London: Dent. 1923); as *It Is So (If You Think So)*, Arthur Livingston, in Eric Bentley, *Naked Masks* (New York: Dutton, 1952); Eric Bentley (New York: Colombia University Press, 1954); Frederick May, *Right You Are! (If You Think So) and Two Other Plays* (London: Penguin, 1962).

A group of bourgeois citizens in a small town are concerned about the behaviour of a family that has just arrived from another village devastated by a recent earthquake. The problem concerns the apparent cruelty of Signor Ponza towards his mother-in-law, Signora Frola, for the old lady does not live with her daughter and son-in-law and appears to be denied access to their home. Despite the advice of Laudisi, one of Pirandello's typical commentator figures, the citizens determine to discover the truth of this situation. Signor Ponza tells them that his mother-in-law is mad, that his first wife, her daughter, is dead, and that he now lives with his second wife who is no relation to Signora Frola. This explanation is shattered by a visit from Signora Frola, who claims that Signor Ponza is mad and that she and her daughter have agreed to maintain the fiction of the second marriage because he has become convinced that his imaginary first wife is dead. By the end of Act One, two conflicting claims have been established, both presented with equal conviction. The next two acts follow the attempts to prove the veracity of one or other of the cases, though Laudisi continues to express his cynical belief in the impossibility of discovering a single, coherent truth. At the conclusion of the play, a woman, dressed in black and veiled, appears. She is Signora Ponza, the woman who holds the key to the puzzle. But when she is asked who she is and which story is the true one, she replies that she is both Signora Frola's daughter and Signor Ponza's wife. She is whoever they believe her to be. The play ends with Laudisi's mocking laughter.

In this play Luigi Pirandello has shown a rare courage, he has tackled insuperable problems and overcome them. The philosopher has overcome them with a touch of cunning. Let us say he is wrong — let's admit that truth can be uncovered — but he has so skilfully slammed the doors in all our faces, producing like a conjuror madness, an earthquake and all kinds of other extraordinary things that even if truth is alive and kicking somewhere, it simply could not appear before us.

But the playwright has fulfilled the miracle of giving life, warmth and a strong, passionate dramatic quality to abstract ideas. He has miraculously transformed a philosophical viewpoint into a convincing theatrical experience. . . .

The audience was somewhat stunned by such an unusual play. They found themselves having to deal not only with facts but also with ideas and this kind of encounter is rare indeed in today's theatre.

But the skill of the writer won them over. The applause and curtain calls were long and frequent. Maria Melato and Ruggero Lupi's splendid performances resulted in applause that stopped the show. Annibale Betrone provided the right ironic flavour for the character of Laudisi. This was a very difficult play to perform, but the Talli Company, with only a few minor flaws, played it perfectly.

Renato Simoni, *Il Corriere della Sera*, 19 June 1918

'What do the characters do on stage?' I was asked by a famous actor who was worried at the absence in the script of all allusions to eating, drinking and smoking and the various activities which his naturalistic technique would be helpless without. I do not believe the answer is to insert them; they contribute nothing. 'Necessary' means 'necessary to the play as Pirandello conceived it', a classic comedy, an elemental tragedy, a slender thriller — anything but a piece of genre painting. What do these people do? They gossip. The furniture of gossip is — the chair. It therefore seemed to me in keeping with Pirandello's almost fanatic lean-mindedness to provide the actors with nothing but chairs. Lester Polakov, our designer, wished to fill the stage with monstrous chairs, their backs five or six feet high, so the actors would spend the evening threading their way through a forest of furniture. The high backs would mask so much of the stage that the 'blocking' problem would be enormous. But some day the idea should be tried.

Eric Bentley, describing his own production of 1952, in the Introduction to his translation of the play (1954), reprinted in *The Pirandello Commentaries*

Cap and Bells (Il berretto a sonagli)

Play in two acts.

First production: in Sicilian dialect, entitled *A birritta cu' i ciancianeddi*, Teatro Nazionale, Rome, 27 June 1917 (Angelo Musco's Company); first Italian-language version, Teatro Argentina, Rome, Apr. 1928 (Luigi Pirandello's Company).

Revivals: Teatro Odeon, Milan, 5 Nov. 1936 (Compagnia del Teatro Umoristico of the De Filippo brothers); Teatro della Cometa, Rome, May 1961 (dir. Diego Fabbri).

First British production: Civic Theatre, Leeds, 20 Jan. 1958 (trans. and

dir. Frederick May).
First published: Noi e il mondo, Rome, 1 Aug.-1 Sept. 1918; also in
    Maschere nude, Vol. III (Milan: Treves, 1920).
Translation: Frederick May, unpublished.

Beatrice, a bourgeois Sicilian wife, is intensely jealous of her husband, and when the play begins she is revealed to be on the point of committing an act that will expose her husband's affair with another man's wife and enable her to leave him. She is warned against taking desperate measures by her confidantes, but goes ahead with her plan regardless. She suspects her husband of having an affair with Nina, the young wife of Ciampa, one of her husband's employees, and her plan is to send Ciampa to the city on an errand, thus leaving the way clear for the lovers to meet and then to arrange for them to be discovered in flagrante. She sends for Ciampa, a clownish figure of grotesquely comic ugliness, who behaves with the utmost propriety, even agreeing to go to Palermo on his master's wife's whim: but before he goes he insists on locking his wife in the house and leaving the keys with Beatrice. She is appalled by this, but agrees when Ciampa offers her the intolerable alternative of having his wife, her rival, to stay with her overnight. In Act Two the repercussions of Beatrice's scheme are beginning to be felt. Her husband has indeed been discovered with Nina, though in circumstances that are not quite as compromising as Beatrice had hoped for, and the small town is stunned by the scandal. Beatrice's mother, Assunta, comes to remonstrate, but the climax comes, as in Act One, with a scene between Beatrice and Ciampa, who comes to confront her with her unfeeling behaviour towards him. It begins to emerge that Ciampa has known of his wife's infidelity, but has chosen to keep up appearances, and now Beatrice's rash actions have swept those appearances away. The only way out for him to redeem his honour is to kill Beatrice's husband and Nina, or for Beatrice to pretend to be mad so that the whole matter can be hushed up and forgotten. Beatrice at first refuses, but then starts to shout like a lunatic to create an impression of madness when she too perceives that this is the only way to avoid more drastic steps. The play ends with Ciampa alone on stage, 'laughing horribly in rage, savage delight and despair all at the same time'.

As for Eduardo (De Filippo) it is impossible to describe how he gradually made his mild mannered reasoning become more frantic, and how he shifted his weakness, his humiliation and his fragility of being the wretched man for whom nobody could feel any pity onto the tragic plane.

His face seemed to turn pallid then light up again hectically, and the despair in his voice sometimes made him hoarse, and then it would tremble with unshed tears. This was a performance that marks a watershed in Eduardo's life and shows that he has reached the heights of complexity and wonder.

Renato Simoni, *Il Corriere della Sera*, 26 Mar. 1936

The Jar (La giara)

One-act play for several actors.

First production: in Sicilian dialect, as *A Giarra*, Teatro Nazionale, Rome, 9 July 1917 (Angelo Musco's Company).

Revivals: Piccolo Teatro dell città di Milano, 27 Jan. 1954 (dir. Giorgio Strehler).

First British production: BBC Television, 28 Oct. 1937 (trans. Arthur Livingston).

First published: as a short story, *Il Corriere della Sera*, Milan, 20 Oct. 1909; as a play, in *Maschere nude*, Vol. XII, second edition (Florence: Bemporad, 1925).

Translations: Arthur Livingston, *Pirandello's One-Act Plays* (New York: Dutton, 1928); William Murray, *Pirandello's One-Act Plays* (New York: Doubleday, 1964).

Don Lolò, a Sicilian landowner, has bought a magnificent new jar for the olive oil that his team of workers will produce after the harvest. As the workers talk, it becomes clear that Don Lolò is a hard man, and when the jar is found to be broken in two everyone is terrified of his anger. Don Lolò demands that the culprit owns up, but everyone denies any knowledge of the breakage, suggesting that the jar may have been defective in the first place. Zio Dima, an old hunchback tinker, is sent for, since he is famous for repairing breakages with his powerful cement.

Don Lolò is sceptical at first, but Zio Dima sets to work and soon repairs the broken jar. However, in order to mend it he has first climbed inside it, as he usually does, but since this jar has an unusually narrow mouth, he is unable to climb out again. Negotiations begin between Zio Dima inside and Don Lolò outside. Don Lolò will agree to break the jar and let Zio Dima out if Zio Dima agrees to pay for the damage. Zio Dima there-fore refuses to come out of the jar and refuses also to pay Don Lolò rent for staying in it. Don Lolò is eventually persuaded to pay Zio Dima for the work he has done, and hands the money into the jar, expecting that he will eventually be able to claim it all back as compensation when Zio Dima finally gives up and is forced to smash his way out. But Zio Dima uses some of the money to throw a party for the workers, and the noise of their celebrations so infuriates Don Lolò that he rushes out of his house and kicks the jar down the hill. The jar breaks, Zio Dima comes out and is carried off in triumph by the workers, shouting that he has won as the landowner loses not only the jar and the cash he has paid out, but also loses face because he has been the one to give in first and the responsibility for breaking the jar is his alone.

The Pleasure of Honesty
(Il piacere dell'onestà)

First production: Teatro Carignano, Turin, 27 Nov. 1917 (Ruggero Ruggeri's Company).

Revivals: Teatro Argentina, Rome, March-April 1927 (Pirandello's Company); Radiotelevisione Italiana, 1955 (with Luigi Cimara).

First British production: Cambridge Amateur Dramatic Club, 15 June 1926; BBC Third Programme, 25 March 1956 (trans. Frederick May, adapted Helena Wood).

First published: Noi e il mondo, Rome, 1 Feb.-1 Mar. 1918; also in *Maschere nude* (Milan: Treves, 1918).

Translations: Arthur Livingston, in *Each in His Own Way and Two Other Plays* (London: Dent, 1924); William Murray, *To Clothe the Naked and Two Other Plays* (New York: Dutton, 1962).

Agata Renni, a respectable unmarried woman, is pregnant by Fabio Colli, a nobleman unhappily married but unable to obtain a divorce from his wife. The play opens with Agata's mother and Fabio's cousin, Maurizio, discussing their plans to resolve the scandalous situation. Maurizio has a bankrupt friend, Angelo Baldovino, and has persuaded him to marry Agata in return for large sums of money. When Baldovino appears, however, the situation becomes more complex, because he agrees to the bargain on very precise terms. He asks Fabio all kinds of leading questions, pointing out that if he is to become a husband and a father to maintain respectability, he has a right to honest answers from the man who has caused the problem in the first place. Agata is at first appalled by the idea of an arranged marriage, but she eventually agrees, and backs up her husband when, in Act Two, Baldovino refuses to allow the baby to be baptized at home, insisting on a public church ceremony — against the wishes of the family, who wanted the event to pass unobtrusively. By Act Three, the collusion between husband and wife is apparent. Fabio tries to trick Baldovino into a crooked deal so that he can be accused of theft, leaving the coast clear for Fabio and Agata to be together, since adultery is less scandalous than unmarried motherhood. But Agata has become more than a wife in name and her feelings for Fabio have changed. Baldovino too is unable to maintain the mask of husband of convenience. At the end of the play Agata declares her commitment to her husband and makes an effective statement of love to Baldovino. Baldovino likewise opens his own heart and, as the curtain falls, Baldovino is in tears of joy and Agata gives him her handkerchief in a symbolic act of sharing. The play ends happily.

But It's Not Serious
(Ma non è una cosa seria)

First production: Teatro Rossini, Leghorn, 22 Nov. 1918 (Emma Gramatica's Company).
Revivals: Italian Television, Oct. 1935 (dir. Mario Landi); Teatro Eliseo, Rome, 1956-57 (dir. Luigi Squarzina).

First British production: as *It's Only a Joke*, Sandeman Hall,
    Edinburgh, 23 Aug. 1958 (trans. Frederick May).
Film version: 1936 (dir. Mario Camerini; with Vittorio de Sica).
First published: in *Maschere nude*, Vol. II (Milan: Treves, 1919).
Translation: Frederick May, unpublished.

Gasparina Toretta, a shabby woman in her late twenties who works in a boarding house, lives a dismal existence with no hope of change. In the first act of the play her situation is made clear by the satirical portraits of some of the frightful guests at the boarding house, of whom only old Signor Barranco is a reasonable human being. Into this environment comes Memmo Speranza (a symbolic name, meaning hope) with a friend, Vico. Memmo enjoys life to the full, and decides on a crazy practical joke that might also serve his own ends. He announces that he wants to marry Gasparina, and, since nobody could possibly take such a marriage seriously, he will be able to carry on with his bachelor existence with a wife as a deterrent to prevent any other women trying to catch him. Gasparina is astonished but finally agrees, and the two enter into this bizarre marriage pact, going through the ceremony but agreeing to live separate lives. However, marriage does wonders for Gasparina, who begins to look young and beautiful again, so that old Signor Barranco wants her to leave Memmo and the sham marriage and marry him instead. But Memmo falls genuinely in love with Gasparina and the play ends happily with the two lovers able at last to live together, once Signor Barranco has left. What began as only a joke has become something very serious indeed — a true and honest marriage.

The Rules of the Game
(Il giuoco delle parti)

First production: Teatro Quirino, Rome, 6 Dec. 1928 (Ruggero
    Ruggeri's Company; with Vera Vergani).
Revivals: Teatro Argentina, Rome, Apr. 1927 (Luigi Pirandello's
    Company); Teatro Eliseo, Rome, Nov. 1965 (De Lullo-Falck-Valli-
    Albani Company); Yvonne Arnaud Theatre, Guildford, 10 July 1982

(trans. Robert Rietti and Noel Cregeen, dir. Anthony Quayle; with Leonard Rossiter).

First British production: BBC Third Programme, 29 Mar. 1953 (trans. Robert Rietti and Noel Cregeen).

First British stage production: Arts Theatre, London, 13 Jan. 1955.

Published: 1-16 Jan. 1919, *Nuova antologia*, Rome; also in *Maschere nude*, Vol. II (Milan: Treves, 1919).

Translations: Robert Rietti, in E. Martin Browne, ed., *Luigi Pirandello: Three Plays* (Penguin, 1959); Robert Rietti and Noel Cregeen, in John Linstrum, ed., *Three Plays* (London: Methuen, 1985).

Leone Gala, a typical Pirandellian rationalist, appears to condone the affair his wife Silia is having with Guido. Leone and Silia are separated, but he still visits her every day and she claims that he will not allow her to be truly free. As Leone is leaving, Silia throws an egg at him from the window, but accidentally hits someone else, one of four young men looking for a call-girl named Pepita. The four young men are all drunk and mistake the egg-throwing as a gesture of invitation. They come up to Silia's apartment and she plays along with them just long enough to discover the name of one of them. Then she calls in her maid and other neighbours and claims they have assaulted her and must be made to apologize publicly. In Act Two, Silia engineers a duel between Leone and one of the young men, in hopes that Leone will be killed and she will be free from him. But the relationship between husband and wife is a complex one, and both move towards each other as they confess to the feelings of deep pain they both feel in life, while Leone says that the only way he can cope with this is by shutting himself off from his true feelings. He appears not to care about Silia at all and seems unmoved by the oncoming duel: but in Act Three that changes. Leone refuses to fight and compels Guido to do so in his stead. When Silia arrives and realizes what Leone has done, how he has changed the rules of the game to his own advantage, Leone drops his mask of indifference and reveals that he has been deeply hurt by Silia's affair and has done this to punish her and her lover. The play ends with Guido mortally wounded offstage while, as Silia runs out to him, Leone remains motionless, stripped of all his protective coverings, completely alone.

I didn't win, but I didn't lose either. *Il giuoco delle parti* was received with hostility by an uncomprehending audience in Act One, but the response was warmer for the second and third acts and aroused enormous discussion.

I know I have created a serious piece of work and so all this noise has not bothered me in the slightest. . . .

Tonight they are doing the play again, but another performance has already been announced for Sunday; that's a sign that the producer doesn't believe the play will be a success. . . .

Ruggeri loves his part and thinks that *Il giuoco delle parti* is my best play yet.

Luigi Pirandello,
letter to his son, Stefano, 8 Dec. 1918

Pirandello's *The Rules of the Game* — pretty hot stuff, considering it was written and presented in Catholic Rome as long ago as 1918 — is a sour blackish eternal triangle comedy which ends with a sting in the tail, or in this case, a bullet in the heart. It is a neat idea, really. The adulterous wife engineers a pistol duel of honour between a crack marksman and her defenceless, detested husband, so that the husband should die and get out of her hair. The husband accepts and chooses his wife's lover as his second. At the appointed hour our hero sleeps late, rises to announce he has no intention of fighting anyone, and eats an egg for breakfast. The lover is honour bound to take the husband's place in the duel. Instead of wife getting rid of husband, husband gets rid of lover.

The whole cynical absurdity is presented by the Compagnia dei Giovani as part of the World Theatre Season. The production is expertly wry throughout, with two highly sophisticated performances by the beauteously-boned Rosella Falk, as the restless and capricious wife, and by Romolo Valli, as the husband whose calm cunning give him the final triumph. Pre-dating Antonioni's cinema dissection of world-weary dolce vita Roman society by some forty years, *The Rules of the Game* covers the same sick, slick territory where boredom is a way of life and life itself just a bed of neuroses. Miss Falk is dressed in some splendidly lurid outfits designed by Pier Luigi Pizzi, who seems to have been inspired by the portraits of Van Dongen and the Dick Tracey comic strip.

Herbert Kretzmer, *Daily Express*, 12 Nov. 1965

Paul Scofield plays Leone in the National Theatre's production. As far as it goes, his performance is masterly. Starting from a voice, drily deliberate, held at arm's length from all emotion, he floats his words out with the watchful detachment of a man blowing smoke rings. Not until the second act, when he's finally alone with his wife, does a tiny smile betray that there's someone left alive under the rubble of blasted pride. He proves that, of all British actors, he's the one best equipped to play Pirandello's reflective, saturnine, fatalistic heroes — he must have been a magnificent television Enrico IV.

But he's simply too distinguished, too indestructibly, sadly civilized, to capture the clowning humiliation of Leone. Even in his idiotic chef's hat and apron, beating eggs under the bullying eye of his manservant, he's unmistakably master of himself and the stage. That may be as it should be, but it needs to be hidden from the audience. Not for a moment could you believe in him as a victim.

As Silia, Joan Plowright is cast equally against the grain. Feeling continually struggles to break through the caricatured shallowness of the character's restless posturing. Still, it's a skilled and very funny performance, serving the play better in its way than Scofield's unbendingly serious one. Preening herself like a bridling osprey, fluttering huge lashes above a great crushed raspberry pout, she flounces through the part like Minnie Mouse imitating one of Bette Davis's sulking temptresses, keeping the farcical half of the evening spiritedly afloat.

The rest of the cast are adequate, and Enrico Job's florid art nouveau designs have the right note of self-parody. But it seemed symptomatic that, although the programme contains a note on duelling, nowhere does it explain for English audiences the code of honour's crucial article that, if a principal does not appear, his second is bound to take his place. Somewhere along the line, in similar fashion, the production misses Pirandello's point.

Ronald Bryden, *The Observer*, 20 June 1970

Rossiter's humour, ambiguity and inscrutability kept the tragedy light. When urged in Act Three to hurry to his duel by the immaculate Barelli (Jeremy Hawk) and a suitably anxious Doctor Spiga (Peter Bennett), both masquerading with due agitation and in the Italian manner, this Leone stood bemusedly picking the rheum from his eyes, examining his findings with most of his attention, and only just managing to return at his leisure to what appeared to the others to be the matter in hand. His was a wry and rueful self-deprecating performance, affording a myriad fleeting glimpses of unacknowledged and unnamed emotions, grazed against and shied away from, but which treacherously persisted in invading the indifferent mask. At moments he seemed to be thinking aloud. His prosaic delivery was so true that one was not always sure if it was Leonard or Leone speaking, as he chatted lightly of his pursuit of inward emptiness, his professed defence against the pain that could be read in his face. There was a moment in the third act in which, sitting on a table behind Silia, he momentarily reached out a hand towards her and then thought better of it, summing up in a half-gesture the very nub of Pirandello's vision of humanity endlessly torn between thought and feeling, mask and face.

The Yearbook of the British Pirandello Society, No. 3, 1983

The Grafting (L'innesto)

First production: Teatro Manzoni, Milan, 29 Jan. 1919 (Virgilio Talli's Company).
Revivals: Teatro Argentina, Rome, 8 Mar 1928 (Luigi Pirandello's Company).
First British production: Institute of Contemporary Arts, London, May 1957 (trans. Robert Rietti).
First published: in *Maschere nude*, Vol. IV (Milan: Treves, 1921).
Translation: Robert Rietti, unpublished.

Laura has been happily married to Giorgio for seven years, although they have no children. When the play opens, Laura's family and friends are discussing this while Laura is out sketching. But the conversation is interrupted by news of a crisis, and Laura is carried in — semi-conscious, having been brutally raped in the park. When Giorgio hears about this, he is filled with rage and resentment and rejects his wife, being less concerned for what she has suffered than for his own sense of outrage. He tries to leave his wife, but is still in love with her and cannot go. When Laura discovers that she is pregnant, probably as a result of the rape, Giorgio is even more appalled, but Laura insists on keeping the child. She talks to an old gardener, who explains the principle of grafting plants to her — grafting will take if the plant is in sap, that is, in a state of love. Laura takes this as a symbol of her own life. Since she loved only Giorgio, the child must be his, regardless of biological paternity. Giorgio cannot accept this, and so Laura tells him she is going to leave him and bring up the child alone. At this point Giorgio is overwhelmed by the strength of Laura's love, and the play ends with husband and wife in each other's arms.

The Licence (La patente)

One-act play for seven actors.

First production: in Sicilian dialect, as *A patenti*, Teatro Argentina, Rome, 19 Feb. 1919 (Teatro Mediterraneo Company, dir. Nino Martoglio).

Revivals: Piccolo Teatro della Città di Milano, 30 Jan. 1954 (dir. Giorgio Strehler); Radiotelevisione Italiana, 1959 (with Mario Scaccia).

First published: as a short story, *Il Corriere della Sera,* Milan, 9 Aug. 1911; as a play, *Rivista d'Italia,* Rome, 31 Jan. 1918; also in *Maschere nude,* Vol. III (Milan: Treves, 1920).

Translations: Elizabeth Abbott, in *Pirandello's One-Act Plays* (New York: Dutton, 1928); William Murray, *Pirandello's One-Act Plays* (New York: Doubleday, 1964).

Judge D'Andrea is defending a case that he feels is doomed. He is defending Rosario Chiarchiaro, a man whom everyone believes can cast the Evil Eye on other people. Chiarchiaro is bringing a libel suit against the mayor's son for making the sign against the Evil Eye when he walked past. So great is the horror that Chiarchiaro arouses in the village, that even the other judges leap backwards and make the sign against the Evil Eye when D'Andrea mentions Chiarchiaro's name. Rosinella, Chiarchiaro's daughter, comes in secret to talk to the judge, to tell him about the family's plight, for nobody will employ Chiarchiaro and his family are in desperate straits. Then Chiarchiaro himself comes, bearded and wild looking, made up to look as sinister as possible. He tells D'Andrea — the only person who does not seem to be gripped with superstitious fear — that he has given evidence to the other side so that they will win the case against him. D'Andrea is perplexed, but Chiarchiaro explains the bitter logic of the situation: since he is unemployable as things stand, he wants the power of his Evil Eye to be legally recognized in the courts, because then he will be able to earn a living by being paid to keep away from people in case he brings bad luck. D'Andrea is filled with pity for Chiarchiaro, but at that moment a gust of wind bangs the shutter and knocks over a birdcage, killing D'Andrea's beloved pet goldfinch. As the judge's colleagues rush in, Chiarchiaro shouts in triumph that he is responsible for this latest evil event. As they all back away from him, he demands protection money from them, saying he will keep away from them and their families if paid to do so. He has found a way of earning his living, and once the trial proves him guilty of having the power of the Evil Eye, he will effectively have been granted a licence to blackmail his superstitious neighbours.

Man, Beast, and Virtue
(L'uomo, la bestia, e la virtù)

First production: Teatro Olimpia, Milan, 2 May 1919 (Antonio Gandusio's Company).

Revivals: Teatro Valle, Rome, Nov. 1948 (De Filippo's Company).

First British productions: New College Dramatic Society, Oxford, 27 May 1957 (trans. Frederick May); BBC Third Programme, 14 July 1957 (trans. Edward Eager, adapted Helena Wood); Theatre Royal, Stratford, 8 Jan. 1958 (trans. Eager and Wood, Theatre Workshop Company, dir. Frances Garnick).

First US production: as *Say It With Flowers*, Garrick Theatre, New York, 3 Dec. 1926 (trans. Alice Rohe).

Film version: 1957 (dir. Steno; with Totò, Viviane Romance, and Orson Welles).

First published: Commedia, Milan, 10 Sept. 1919; also in *Maschere nude*, Vol. V, second edition (Florence: Bemporad, 1922).

Translations: Frederick May, 1957; Edward Eager, 1958, unpublished.

Paolino, a private tutor of great propriety, is in love with Signora Perrella, the mother of one of his pupils, Nono. While he is trying to instil some learning into two blockheaded pupils, Signora Perella and her son arrive, and she communicates by sign language to Paolino the fact that she is pregnant. An immensely respectable woman, she is married to a sailor who already has a second family elsewhere, and whose gross behaviour has killed off any love she may once have had for him. Perella, in turn, no longer finds his wife sexually attractive, and deliberately avoids sleeping with her when he is at home, claiming that he cannot afford the risk of having any more children. As he is about to come home from a journey, Paolino and Signora Perella decide that the only course of action to hide the truth from the world is to make Perella sleep with her so that later she can claim that the expected child is his. Paolino and Signora Perella, deeply in love and clinging to appearances and proprieties, are therefore forced into a grotesque subterfuge. He obtains some cakes from a doctor friend that have been treated with an aphrodisiac, and then helps Signora Perella to tart herself up, with a low neckline and exaggerated make-up. Paolino and Signora Perella make a pact: if the aphrodisiac works she will place a vase on the balcony as a sign that all is well. As Act Two draws to a close, it seems very unlikely that the plan will work and the crudity of Perella is contrasted with the meekness of his rejected wife. But the play ends on a note of farce, for when Paolino comes to visit, he finds his beloved looking utterly exhausted and placing not one, but five vases in a row for him to see.

Frankly, we had hoped that by now husbands could hold our interest with more important matters: but here is Luigi Pirandello harping on the same old tune. . . . The audience reacted more than once to this lack of taste. . . . The proceedings of the evening were quite wretched; there were three conflicting calls after the first act, open disapproval after the second, and protests during the third act, the last words of which were drowned by loud shouting. . . .

Last night at the Teatro Olimpico the voice of the prompter could be heard better than anyone else.

Renato Simoni, *Il Corriere della Sera*, 5 May 1919

All for the Best (Tutto per bene)

First production: Teatro Quirino, Rome, 2 March 1920 (Ruggero Ruggeri's Company).
Revivals: Teatro Argentina, Rome, Apr. 1927 (Luigi Pirandello's Company); Teatro Eliseo, Rome, Nov. 1965 (De Lullo-Falck-Valli-Albani Company).
First British production: BBC Third Programme, 24 Nov. 1953 (trans. and adapted Henry Reed).
First published: Maschere nude, Vol. I, second edition (Florence: Bemporad, 1920).

Translation: Henry Reed, in E. Martin Browne, ed., *Right You Are if You Think So and Two Other Plays* (Harmondsworth: Penguin, 1960).

When the play opens, an elderly woman and her son are arriving as uninvited guests at the wedding of Palma Lori to a marquis. The elderly woman is Palma's grandmother, but she has never seen her grand-daughter because of a family rift. Palma's mother, Silvia, died some sixteen years previously, but had broken off relations with her own mother when she married Martino Lori, a poor but honest man who has made a daily pilgrimage to the cemetery to visit his beloved wife's grave. When Martino finds his detested mother-in-law in the house, old skeletons are rattled in the cupboards, but Palma views it all with amusement and her contempt for her father is strikingly obvious. She shows far more affection for Senator Salvo Manfroni, the man who has helped her financially and given a decent job to Martino. In Act Two, when the young couple are settled in their lavish new home, the truth behind Palma's opinions is revealed. Palma knows that Martino is not her real father, and that her mother had been having an affair with Senator Manfroni. But, crucially, she and everyone else believes that Martino also knows this, and so they all have contempt for what they see as his cynical self-advancement, profiting from the generosity of his dead wife's lover and making his daily hypocritical pilgrimage to the cemetery to keep up appearances. Palma lets the cat out of the bag when she calls Manfroni her father and Martino is suddenly faced with the appalling truth that not only is Palma not his daughter, but all his life has been based on a lie. His beloved Silvia never loved him, and for sixteen years everyone has seen him as a figure of contempt. Martino is horrified by this, but the others are equally horrified to discover that he did not know the truth. Palma begins at last to feel affection for him and, although not her biological father, he earns the respect of a father from her by his honesty. In a final bitter twist of the knife, Martino exposes Manfroni as a fraud who owes his reputation as a scientist to some stolen notes. Martino kept silent so as not to hurt Manfroni, but now he threatens to publish and expose him. Manfroni dares him to do *this, and Martino has to acknowledge that it would only be his word against that of a powerful man, and he would never be believed. But the play ends on an optimistic note, for Palma now openly admits that she loves Martino as a father, and that in losing everything else in his life he has at least gained the affection of a daughter. It has all been for the best after all.*

Ruggero Ruggeri as Martino Lori did not convince me at all. He is unquestionably a first-class actor, but he is an actor whose passion does not go very deep. His passion does not tear at him.

The final piece of news is this: we have a new Pirandello. Yes indeed! Who would have thought it? Who would have thought that Luigi Pirandello could have learned how to write plays? That is, would have learned to write in the manner of Augier, Dumas, Sardou, all the rest of them? But that is the case here.

Marco Praga, 'Un Pirandello nuovo',
L'Illustrazione Italiana, Milan, 10 May 1920

I simply cannot understand why (and last night in the stalls of the Quirino at the start of the play there were some whisperings to this effect) this play is supposed to have unusual characteristics and meanings for a Pirandello work.

It seemed to me, for better or worse, that this was one of the most typically Pirandellian products. As I have said on more than one occasion, in a good many plays by Pirandello, one starts off with a situation that is quite arbitrarily contrived and complicated and enables the author to move a few more or less unpleasant puppets around through a sequence of rapid, dull scenes, to the point (which almost always comes too late) when something snaps and the puppets turn into human beings, and a trickle or a flood of feeling uncovers the secret torment of the objects we have hitherto perceived as stiff and wooden.

Silvio d'Amico, *L'Idea Nazionale,* 4 March 1920

As Before, Better Than Before
(Come prima, meglio di prima)

First production: Teatro Goldoni, Venice, 24 Mar. 1920 (Ferrero-Celli-Paoli Company).

First US production: as *Floriani's Wife,* 44th St. Theatre, New York,
   1 Oct. 1923 (trans. Anna Sprague Macdonald).
Film version: entitled *This Love of Ours,* 1945 (dir. William Dieterle,
   adapted by Bruce Manning, John Klorer, and Leonard Lee).
First published: Maschere nude, Vol. II, second edition (Florence:
   Bemporad, 1921).
Translation: Anna Sprague Macdonald, unpublished.

Fulvia Gelli, a woman who left her husband and daughter some thirteen years ago, has tried to kill herself and been saved by her husband, Silvio. He falls in love with her again, and when the play opens Fulvia rejects her present lover Marco Mauri, in order to accompany Silvio back to his home. The only condition is that she will assume another name and pretend to their daughter Livia that she is Silvio's second wife. Livia has always been told that her mother was dead, and she continues to worship the memory of that lost, idealized mother, so Silvio and Fulvia decide to keep up this fiction. Marco is horrified by Fulvia's decision, since he has given up his own family and his position for her, but she is adamant. In Act Two she is installed again in Silvio's home, but encounters the hostility of Livia, who perceives her as supplanting her real mother. The crisis between mother and daughter is precipitated by the arrival of Fulvia's aunt, Zia Ernestina, and by the birth of Fulvia's second daughter. In the final moments of the play Fulvia tells Livia the truth — the woman she hates as an unworthy stepmother is in fact her real mother, and the illusion of a perfect mother is shattered forever. Livia faints and Silvio tells Fulvia that she must go. Fulvia prepares to leave with Marco and her baby, but insists that she will also take Livia with her. Things cannot be as they have been before, but by finally being honest, perhaps they will be better than before.

Chee-Chee (Cècè)

First production: according to Mondadori, Teatro Orfeo, Rome, 14 Dec.
   1915 (Teatro a Sezioni Company); according to Leonardo Bragaglia,
   Teatro del Gran Casino di San Pellegrino Terme, 10 July 1920.

First British production: Institute of Education Theatre, London, 12 Nov. 1948 (trans. Frederick May).
First US production: Playhouse Repertory Company, New York, 10 July 1953 (trans. Elizabeth Abbott).
First published: La Lettura, Milan, Oct. 1913.
Translations: Elizabeth Abbott, *Pirandello's One-Act Plays* (New York: Dutton, 1928); William Murray, *Pirandello's One-Act Plays* (New York: Doubleday, 1964).

Cècè is a young man about town, whose nickname recalls the noise birds make as they chatter, a parallel that he draws when visited by his acquaintance, the wealthy Squatriglia, in his first–class hotel room in Rome. Cècè cunningly convinces Squatriglia, who is not very bright, to help him trick Nada, his lady friend, into returning three compromising IOUs that he has given her. When Nada telephones, Cècè makes Squatriglia answer and then when she arrives at the hotel, Cècè hides. Squatriglia puts the plan into action, and manages to convince Nada that Cècè has disgraced his whole family and that if the business of the IOUs becomes public it will hurt a great many people. Nada believes the story and hands them over. Squatriglia leaves, and Cècè comes out of hiding. He pretends that Squatriglia was a moneylender, and accuses Nada of being gullible. Nada's feelings of outrage against Cècè, stirred up by Squatriglia's story, disappear, and the play ends with Nada and Cècè reconciled. Cècè has kept his mistress and has managed to gull her out of the money he owed her as well.

Signora Morli, One and Two
(La Signora Morli, una e due)

First production: Teatro Argentina, Rome, 12 Nov. 1920 (Emma Gramatica's Company).
Revivals: Teatro Eden, Milan, 10 Apr. 1926 (Luigi Pirandello's Company; with Marta Abba); Teatro Odeon, Milan, 7 Oct. 1940 (Elsa Merlini-Renato Cialente Company).
First published: Maschere nude, Vol. VI (Florence: Bemporad, 1922).

Translation: as *Mrs. Morli, One and Two*, Helen Jerome, unpublished.

Evelina Morli, wife of Ferrante Morli, is abandoned by him with her little son, Aldo. Lello Carpani, a lawyer, falls in love with her and she goes to live with him, eventually giving him a daughter, Titti. The play begins fourteen years after Evelina has been abandoned, and Aldo is now a young man. Ferrante, under an assumed name, arrives at Lello's house after many years in America, hoping to see his son. Lello does not recognize him, but when Evelina appears she does, and is horrified at the idea that he might want to take his son away with him. Aldo discovers the truth and decides to leave with Ferrante, while Evelina stays with Lello and their daughter. In Act Two, Evelina is with Aldo and Ferrante, after they have sent her a telegram saying that Aldo is ill and needs her to be with him. Evelina finds that once back with Ferrante she undergoes a personality change. When they lived together before she felt free and uninhibited, and although during the years with Lello she has lived a quiet, respectable life, once back with Ferrante she rediscovers the hidden part of herself. Ferrante tries to convince her to stay with him, and even Aldo perceives the change in his mother and prefers the more open, carefree side of her. But Evelina's sense of duty to Lello and love for Titti prevails, and she goes back home again, having turned down Ferrante's proposal that they should live together again as man and wife. In Act Three, she has to deal with Lello's desperate jealousy, but she finally convinces him that nothing has happened between her and Ferrante, and that although she is still legally married to Ferrante, she has come back to continue being the dutiful wife and mother Lello has always known and loved.

Six Characters in Search of an Author
(Sei personaggi in cerca d'autore)

First production: Teatro Valle, Rome, 10 May 1921 (Dari Niccodemi's
   Company, with Vera Vergani and Luigi Almirante).
Revivals: Comédie des Champs-Elysées, Paris, 10 Apr. 1923 (dir.

Georges Pitöeff); Teatro Argentina, Rome, May 1923 (Spettacolo
d'Arte Company, dir. Lamberto Picasso); Komödie Teater, Berlin,
30 Dec. 1924 (dir. Max Reinhardt); Teatro Odescalchi, Rome,
May 1925, followed by European tour (Luigi Pirandello's Company);
Teatro Argentina, Rome, 30 Nov. 1936 (Ruggero Ruggeri's
Company); Teatro Nuovo, Milan, Feb. 1942 (dir. Guido Salvini);
Teatro Quirino, Rome, 29 Nov. 1946 (dir. Orazio Costa); Teatro
La Fenice, Venice, Sept. 1948 (Accademia dell'Arte Drammatica
Company, dir. Silvio d'Amico); Teatro dei Satiri, Rome, 23 Oct. 1954
(dir. Franco Castellani); BBC Television, 20 Apr. 1954 (trans.
Frederick May); Phoenix Theatre, New York, 24 Oct. 1955 (adapted
by Tyrone Guthrie and Michael Wagner); City Centre, New York,
26 Apr. 1959 (three-act opera, with libretto by Denis Johnston, music
by Hugo Weisgall); Teatro delle Arti, Rome, 18 Oct. 1960 (dir. Lucio
Chiaravelli); Giardino del Palazzo Reale, Turin, 30 June 1964
(De Lullo-Falck-Valli-Albani Company); National Theatre, London,
Feb. 1987 (dir. Michael Rudman, adapted by Nicholas Wright).
First British production: Kingsway Theatre, London, 26 Feb. 1922
(Stage Society, dir. Theodore Komisarjevsky, trans. Mrs. W. A.
Greene).
First US production: Fulton Theatre, New York, 30 Oct. 1922.
First published: Maschere nude, Vol. III, second edition (Florence:
Bemporad, 1921; revised version, with preface, 1925).
Translations: of the first version, Edward Storer, in *Three Plays*
(London: Dent, 1922), reprinted in Eric Bentley, *Naked Masks*
(New York: Dutton, 1952); Frederick May (London: Heinemann,
1954); John Linstrum (London: Methuen, 1970), reprinted in John
Linstrum, ed., *Three Plays* (London: Methuen, 1985).

---

*The play opens with the illusion of a company in rehearsal,
preparing a production of another of Pirandello's plays,* Il giuoco
delle parti. *The rehearsal is interrupted by the arrival of six
people — the Father, the Mother, the Step-daughter, the Son,
and two small children who do not speak. They claim they have
come to the theatre looking for a means of presenting their
story: they are characters searching for an author. As their story
unfolds, told principally by the Father and the Step-daughter, we
learn that at some time in the past the Mother has gone to live
with another man and had children by him, though whether
because of the Father's cruelty to her or because he simply*

wanted her to be happy is unclear. The Father's version of events is that he loved the Mother, but the Step-daughter depicts him in another light as a disgusting, debauched old man who used to spy on her when she was a child on her way to school. The characters try to persuade the company to act out their story, and in the second act another figure is summoned by them — Madame Pace, the owner of a milliners-cum-brothel where the Step-daughter was working and to which the Father came one afternoon in search of a girl. The incestuous encounter between Father and Step-daughter is interrupted by the Mother's cry of anguish. In the third act the Mother tries in vain to win over the affection of the sullen, angry Son, who has rejected her, but while her attention is focused on him, the little girl drowns in a fountain in the garden and the little boy, who has been the constant object of the Step-daughter's hatred, shoots himself. The Step-daughter flees, and Father, Mother, and Son remain trapped in their misery and grief. The boundary between reality and fiction has broken down, and the Director tries vainly to understand what is going on in his theatre.

It is normally extremely difficult to summarize the plots of Pirandello's plays, because what is important about them is never the crude plot line, nor the facts, nor even the action, but rather the process that develops inside the souls of his characters and which manifests itself through a series of reasoned arguments by which they clarify things for themselves and for others, contriving both to explain to others and win for themselves the spiritual position they have reached or at which they have halted. It would be a foolish, vain undertaking to attempt to summarize the plot of the play which was premiered last night at the Teatro Valle. . . .

Any great work of art, if it appears at all, appears after a lengthy, laborious preceding preparation which is necessary. From today, we can say that Pirandello is most certainly among the leading creators of a new spiritual environment, one of the most deserving precursors of tomorrow's genius if tomorrow ever comes.

The Niccodemi Company successfully overcame the overwhelming difficulties of this stage experiment. Margheri was an excellent Director, Madame Vergani skilfully rendered all that there was of brutal grace and feline lust for revenge in the character of the Step-daughter. This young actress is developing her technique before our eyes and is becoming a strong, intelligent, amazingly versatile actress. Mr. Almirante (who one might have wished a little less servile and downtrodden on occasion) portrayed fairly well the complex, tormented character of the Father. The others were excellent. There were a good many curtain calls at the end of the first act and at the end of the second, when Pirandello was called onto the stage I don't know how many times. But, truth to tell, it was a success imposed by a minority on a bewildered, confused public who were basically trying hard to understand. After the third act, however, the weakest act of all, which ends so absurdly, a storm of protest broke out that the supporters of the work tried bravely to counter. And so ended an evening that really was a battle for all of us, for the author, the public and also for the critics.

Adriano Tilgher, review of Six Characters, 1921

The Stage Society produced a most original play last Monday and acted it extraordinarily well. The play is by Signor Luigi Pirandello, who is one of the leading Italian dramatists and a writer of admirable short stories. It was produced last year in Rome and made a great impression. The Stage Society's programme included a note by A. W. on the play. It was needed; for without some introduction, many of the audience would have been puzzled by this experiment in dramatic form.

It is neither a play within a play, nor yet a play in the making. Rather it is a trial — possibly an indictment — of the modern theatre. The author has created Six Characters and imagined for them a situation of poignant intensity. And then, doubtful of the theatre's adequacy for his intentions, he abandons his play — it is not to be written. But the characters remain; he has endowed them with life and they refuse to relinquish his gift. A theatrical stock company meets to put another Pirandello play into rehearsal, and as they begin their work, the six characters arrive, and demand that their story shall be given the dramatic representation for which it was destined.

What an extraordinary plot for a play! How can a play be made out of such a situation? It certainly required considerable cleverness to do it, but Signor Pirandello is clearly endowed with a quite enormous amount of ingenuity. This is how he did it.

The curtain did not go up. It was up when we assembled; we found ourselves sitting in front of the dark empty stage, and presently, one after the other, a number of actors and actresses, in their everyday clothes, walked on. The humorously strident voice of Mr. Alfred Clark was heard giving directions for a rehearsal, and the lights were turned up. A slightly quarrelsome, snappy chatter followed, and the rehearsal was just getting under way, when at the back of the stage appeared a gloomy procession of figures dressed in deep mourning. An elderly man in immaculate black, a woman, presumably a widow, in streaming weeds, a tiny girl, a young girl about eighteen, a youth, say twenty-two, and a little boy about twelve. These people are 'Characters' in a play Signor Pirandello intended to write.

Desmond McCarthy, *Drama* (London and New York, 1940)

The third production of the season was Reinhardt's most powerful presentation of *Six Characters in Search of an Author* in which Pallenberg, Lucy Hoflich, Gulstorf, Bildt and Diegelmann also played an essential part. We have not seen such consummate ensemble work for many years on the German stage. The more one reflects on it, the clearer it becomes that it was Max Reinhardt rather than Pirandello who was the poet of this performance of a play in the making. Certainly Pirandello's concept, or should one say fantasy, is superb and shatteringly enigmatic. In the middle of a rehearsal of a new play — and so in a setting that fills every theatregoer immediately with a sense of delightful magic, with lights, stage hands, actors in ordinary clothes, stage manager and producer — six characters shuffle onto the stage, an unreal, ghostly line of people: the Father, Mother, the Daughter, the Son, and two small children — figures created by an author but not fully realized. They demand release from their present condition, and their right to live, even if only as a character. They refuse to be turned away. In contrast to the actors, the producer becomes excited by their story and tries to realize it on stage. A dubious undertaking.

But when we read what Pirandello had to say about the play, we immediately notice that he did not see the magnitude and the possibilities of his theme. A romantic play by a anti-romantic author: Reinhardt felt the potential of this piece and offered a master production of his art in which the audience became fully aware of all the horror of this gloomy world. There is a struggle between the Characters (created by an author, who continue to exist even though he has withdrawn his sustaining hand either through lack of interest or lack of ability) with the author, and a struggle between the author and the actors; and from the way this struggle is presented, it becomes apparent that sometimes a higher reality is attributed to the real people (the actors and the actresses) and sometimes to the Characters. Like departed souls in Hades yearning for life-giving blood, these Characters yearn for the dramatic realization of their experience. And out of this predicament there suddenly appears the incarnation of the horrendous figure of the Madame (Marguerite Kupfer) who stands solidly on the stage. All this happens in those regions where the borderline between appearance and reality overlaps, where what is imagination and theatrical creation can be more real than physical reality, and where in order to stay sane, it is necessary to lose one's mind.

The confusion of opposites, of author and actor, who can both destroy and create, of the reality of life and the reality of theatre, rends convention apart and leaves much to think about. In these undefinable spectral regions, Reinhardt gave the best evidence so far in his career of his inexhaustively fertile mind.

Rudolph Pechel, review of Reinhardt's production,
Deutsche Rundschau, 1924

Well, we have all seen the great Pirandello, and discovered that he is, as they say, no chicken. He came on between the first and second acts of his *Sei personaggi*, and made a few exegetic remarks which didn't much help us in the audience, but which absolutely stumped the interpreter. A baffled interpreter was an unhoped for addition to the joy of the evening. 'Mr. Pirandello says,' the poor man would begin, but what it was that Mr. Pirandello said proved nearly always too much for him. The crowded and brilliant house evidently thought this interlude immense fun.

The *Sei personaggi*, it will be remembered, has already been done in English — and in the English fashion — by the Stage Society. It is another, a different, play done in Italian by Italians. Everything is a little 'more so'. The tragic personages are more tragic, the squalid personages more squalid, and the comic remnant more emphatically and volubly comic. Benissimo! . . .

Call it Pirandellism and you have a name for a new theatrical amusement. For it is certainly amusing to see characters disintegrated, as it were, on the stage before you, wondering how much of them is illusion and how much reality, and setting you pondering over these perplexing problems while enjoying at the same time the orthodox dramatic thrill. For, if we have used the word amusing, it must be understood in the widest sense. Nothing could be more impressive than the solemn procession on to the stage of the Six (all in deep black), with their pale masks and their tragic eyes; they seem like some accursed family from the Aeschylan stage. And they are truly tragic in their acting, Marta Abba the daughter and Lamberto Picasso the father. But our last word of commendation must be reserved for that astonishing little silent, immovable mite, N. N.

The Times, 16 June 1925

Signor Pirandello has realized that philosophy has yet another branch — namely, metaphysics — and has sent the drama to school in that faculty. Where the old characters asked 'What is right?' the new ones ask 'What is real?' so that a Pirandello play resolves itself into a dramatized version of a first-year course upon appearance and reality. The author's strength lies not in any philosophical brilliance but in the practical cunning whereby he has made metaphysics actable. A student, for instance, who had begun to explore the devious paths of meaning attached to the word 'reality', might happen to ask himself, 'Is not Mr. Micawber more real than Charles Dickens's father?' On that elementary kind of confusion the play of the six characters has been based. May not the imaginary characters who try and impose themselves upon a play in rehearsal be more 'real' than anybody on the stage? The setting of this question provides a chance for whimsical comings and goings and fantastic contrasts. But the question is not answered and the play, like most elementary investigations of metaphysical tangles, leads nowhere in particular. . . .

The acting tonight seemed, to one judging merely from the translation, to be fully adequate to its theme. Foreign theatres specialize more than our own in the fantastic aspects of the drama, and the contrast of the imaginary characters with the real actors was marked by well-sustained distinction of style. Again, the Roman Art Theatre, like its Moscow namesake, can show the art of ensemble at its highest. The fluidity of the groups and of group-chatter had all the rippling continuity of life and made most English approaches to such effects seem very awkward and still. The two chief parts were played by Lamberto Picasso and Marta Abba with a swift and sweeping intensity that brought the author's speculative method into touch with the normal theatre situation and emotion.

Manchester Guardian, 16 June 1925

Henry IV (Enrico IV)

First production: Teatro Manzoni, Milan, 24 Feb. 1922 (Ruggero
    Ruggeri's Company).
Revivals: Teatro Argentina, Rome, 11 June 1925, followed by European
    tour (Luigi Pirandello's Company); Comédie des Champs Elysées,
    Paris, Feb. 1925 (dir. Georges Pitöeff); Teatro Pirandello, Agrigento,
    Dec. 1946 (with Lamberto Picasso); Teatro Nuovo, Milan, Apr. 1953
    (with Ruggero Ruggeri); Teatro Stabile della Città di Napoli,
    Dec. 1959 (dir. Orazio Costa; with Salvo Randone); Her Majesty's
    Theatre, London, Feb. 1974 (with Rex Harrison).
First British production: Amateur Dramatic Club, Cambridge,
    7 June 1924 (trans. Edward Storer).
First US production: as *The Living Mask*, 44th St. Theatre, New York,
    21 Jan. 1924.

First published: Maschere nude, Vol. IV (Florence: Bemporad, 1922).
Translations: Edward Storer, in *Three Plays* (London: Dent, 1923), and
in Eric Bentley, ed., *Naked Masks* (New York: Dutton, 1952);
Frederick May, in E. Martin Browne, ed., *Three Plays*
(Harmondsworth: Penguin, 1962); as *The Emperor*, Eric Bentley, in
The Genius of the Italian Theatre (New York: Mentor, 1964);
Julian Mitchell (London, Methuen, 1979); and in John Linstrum, ed.,
Three Plays (London: Methuen, 1985).

Some twenty years before the action of the play begins, a group of young aristocrats have staged a masquerade in which each guest chose to appear as a character from history. One of these men, having chosen the part of Emperor Henry IV, fell off his horse, hit his head, and as a result of brain damage caused by the fall has remained since then under the illusion that he is the real Emperor. For twenty years he has been shut away in a country villa, decorated to look like a medieval castle, and the people employed to care for him have had to maintain the fiction of being part of a medieval court. When the play opens, a new servant, Bertoldo, has just arrived and is wearing the wrong costume, having thought that Henry IV was the French Renaissance king of the same name. Shortly afterwards, visitors arrive: Henry's nephew, the Marquis di Nolli, his fiancee Frida, Frida's mother, Matilda, the woman that Henry was formerly in love with, her lover Belcredi, and a psychiatrist. Belcredi views Henry's madness with some cynicism, but Matilde hopes he can still be cured. When Henry appears, a faded, painted figure, he looks to be the personification of madness, but in the word game he plays there are suggestions that he might not be as mad as he wants to seem. In Act Two, the visitors decide to try shock tactics to effect a cure. Frida and De Nolli, younger versions of Matilda and Henry, are to dress in the old masquerade costumes and stand in front of two portraits painted twenty years earlier when Henry was still young and sane. But Henry reveals to his retainers that he is not mad at all; some years earlier he had been miraculously cured and since then has continued to live out a fiction of madness. When the crisis comes in Act Three, Henry is almost driven mad again by seeing what he thinks is the portrait of Matilde come to life. When Belcredi, Henry's old rival, accuses him of play-acting, he takes his revenge, stabbing Belcredi to death. By this action, which is a logical gesture of revindication, Henry signals to the world that he is still in the grip of madness. Having acted in sanity, he is finally perceived as authentically mad, and the play ends with his realizing that he must remain trapped in the role of the mad emperor for the rest of his life.

Much of the meaning of *Henry IV* will depend of course on the actor who does the central character. Mr. Korff is a very good actor indeed in a certain style. He has a fine voice and a good mask in the manner of the Flemish or German schools of painting. But his portrayal of Henry IV lacks most of all distinction and bite. It is too full of sentiment and too short of mental agitation; it has too much nerves and heart and too little brains. The average audience must get the impression from Mr. Korff that we see a man whose life has been fantastically spoiled by the treachery of an enemy, that the fall from his horse began his disaster, which was completed by the infidelity and loose living of the woman he loved. But this weakens the whole drama; the root of the tragic idea was in the man's mind long before the accident; Pirandello makes that clear enough. The playing of this character, which is one of the great roles in modern drama, needs first of all a dark cerebral distinction and gravity; the tragedy, the irony, the dramatic and philosophical theme, depend on that. Mr. Korff has theatrical power and intensity, but too much waggling of his head; he is too grotesque and undignified vocally; he has too little precision and style for the part; and not enough intellectual excitement and ideal poignancy. And the very last moment of the play he loses entirely by the rise that he uses in his voice and by the kind of crying tumult that he creates. . . .

> Stark Young, review of the American premiere,
> reprinted in *Immortal Shadows* (New York, 1948)

It is the tragedy of a man who cherishes a delusion because he is happier in it than in a world that has used him ill. People from the real world outside burst into his dream and shatter it, tearing off the bandages that he has wrapped round his wound, and under the shock he commits a murder. An Italian nobleman playing in a pageant the part of the Emperor Henry IV — the Emperor who was humiliated by the Pope at Canossa — is made mad by an accident, and his madness takes the form of imagining himself to be in reality Henry IV. When we first see him, twenty years after, he is surrounded by a mock Court in his villa. This gives the opportunity for some bright pageantry, delightfully done. He has been sane for years, but, his love having left him in his madness, he has chosen rather to wrap himself in a dream of history than to return to the life of men. His old love with her daughter and her lover arrive at the 'Court' with an alienist (a rich comic character) on the merciful errand of helping the 'madman'. Strange and wonderful things happen. The characters from the outside world fall in with the masquerade to humour him, and he plays up to them, somewhat in the spirit of Hamlet in his scenes with the two courtiers. The motive of his behaviour is perfectly simple — it is love and jealousy mixed with outraged idealism, and the final crash comes when he kills the lover of his countess in a fury at being dragged down from his dream into the agony of things as they are. Then he returns to his dream — 'for ever'.

If there was any need for elucidation in the text — and, as I say, it seems straightforward to the verge of melodrama — the superb acting of Signor Ruggero Ruggeri was, like all great acting, plain as a pikestaff. He left you in no doubt at all. In the earlier part of the play he acts the madman with tragic insight and power, and with restraint one does not always get from Italian actors. He shows you the picture of a tortured soul, playing a part but — like Hamlet again — playing it as an escape from the pressure of torture. There are tones in his voice of singular sweetness in pain. In the next act there is an amazing outburst when he throws off the mask among his 'counsellors', in a sort of spate of intellectual buffoonery, once more reminiscent of the hysteria of Hamlet. Lastly, his mood turns to anger, when he turns on the people from outside and pours out all the stored-up bitterness of his tragedy of lost and betrayed love. No doubt there is more in it than this crude summary would suggest: there is a closely woven network of subtleties, of suggested emotional strains, but no-one of ordinary sensitiveness could miss the fact that Pirandello has put on the stage a great tragic figure and found a great actor to make it live for us.

Manchester Guardian, 20 June 1925

Madness, whether treated poetically as by Shakespeare, or ironically, as by Pirandello, is always a moving spectacle. It becomes terrible in the hands of Signor Ruggero Ruggeri. His voice and glance and gestures hover on the outer edge of the uncanny. When his mind is restored to him he towers superb over the technically sane inferiors — petty in their loves and hates, in their pedantry and folly — who huddle round him. Ruggero Ruggeri is a great actor. And Signor Pirandello, in acknowledging his debt to him in a short curtain-speech, did what we all felt to be not only a graceful but the right thing.

The Times, 19 June 1925

The play takes a full hour to get off the ground; but once it does it soars. What strikes me particularly is its extraordinary resonant modernity; when Henry claims that the madman 'can challenge your logic with a logic of his own' and that the sane man says a thing can't be while the madman says everything can be, we are plunged straight into the world of R. D. Laing. But Pirandello's great gift was to make his philosophy exciting in theatrical terms: last night you could have heard a pin drop at the great moment of revelation when the mad monarch quietly starts to hum the Toreador song from *Carmen* while pulling out a cigar from his eleventh century tunic. And the ending, with real madness closing in once more, is as powerful and inevitable as anything in modern drama.

I only wish Clifford Williams's production fully matched Pirandello's unashamed theatricality: it seems curiously typical that at the end Henry stabs his rival with a tiny dagger rather than the specified sword. But, after a slight initial uncertainty with too many lines sacrificed to a tenor yelp, Rex Harrison gives a masterly performance. Irony and weariness are his forte: and he beautifully conveys the tragedy of a man who has deliberately denied himself life and who has too long preserved his wasteful isolation. And when, asked the identity of his assailant at the pageant, he cries: 'Does it matter who?' his voice rises and falls in an arc of infinite mournful regret. It makes me wish that Harrison, who is finely supported by James Villiers as his peppery rival and Yvonne Mitchell as his ageing mistress, had more often devoted his rueful grave-yard melancholy to the classics.

The Guardian, 21 Feb. 1974

At the Exit (All'uscita)

First production: Teatro Argentina, Rome, 29 Sept. 1922 (Ruggero
    Ruggeri's Company).
First published: Nuova antologia, Rome, 1 Nov. 1916; as a story, in
    E Domani, Lunedi (Milan: Treves, 1917); also in *Maschere nude*
    Vol. IV, fourth edition (Milan: Mondadori, 1949).
Translation: Blanche Valentine Mitchell, in *Pirandello's One-Act Plays*
    (New York: Dutton, 1928); William Murray, *Pirandello's One-Act
    Plays* (New York: Doubleday, 1964).

The setting is a cemetery gate, and the characters are all phantoms. The ghost of the Fat Man and the Philosopher discuss their past lives; the Philosopher is cynically detached

49

about the pain of life and death, while the Fat Man recalls the infidelities of his wife. With the second sight of the dead, the Fat Man predicts that his unfaithful wife will be murdered by her lover, and almost immediately she appears and joins them in the cemetery. A Little Boy comes down the road: he is eating a pomegranate, and when he has finished it, he vanishes. The Philosopher explains that once his last desire (that of eating the pomegranate) has been fulfilled, he will be released. The Murdered Woman breaks down and weeps, and the Fat Man disappears too, having finally seen his unfaithful wife suffer. A group of peasants pass by, and cannot see the phantoms, though a child senses their presence. As the play ends, the Murdered Woman is running hopelessly after the peasant family, doomed to remain at the exit in limbo, with her desire for children unfulfilled, and the Philosopher comments ironically that he will never move anywhere, and will always remain where he is, still reasoning.

The Imbecile (L'imbecille)

First production: Teatro Quirino, Rome, 10 Oct. 1922 (Alfredo Sainati's Company).
First British production: as *The Fool,* Studio Theatre Club at Mahatma Ghandi Assembly Hall, London, 22 Jan. 1956. (trans. Harry McWilliam).
First published: as a short story, *Il Corriere della Sera,* Milan, 11 Sept. 1912; as a play, in *Maschere nude,* Vol. XIX (Florence: Bemporad, 1926).
Translations: Blanche Valentine Mitchell, in *Pirandello's One-Act Plays* (New York: Dutton, 1928); William Murray, *Pirandello's One-Act Plays* (New York: Doubleday, 1964).

The action takes place in a provincial newspaper office. Leopoldo Paroni, the editor, detests his political rival, Guido Mazzarini, and dreams about killing him. The news is brought that a young man, Pulino, suffering from an incurable disease, has killed himself. Leopoldo calls him an idiot and an imbecile for dying this way without having first eliminated Mazzarini,

*and says he would have even paid the young man's fare to Rome
and given him the gun with which to do it. But throughout all
this wild talk, Luca Fazio, another young man who is incurably
ill, has been lying on a couch in the office, listening. When the
other reporters leave, Luca pulls a gun on Leopoldo and tells
him that Guido Mazzarini has paid his fare to come down and
kill Leopoldo, before killing himself. Leopoldo's courage
crumbles, but Luca has no intention of actually killing him.
Instead, Luca wants to expose him as the imbecile, and so he
forces him to write a note stating that he, Leopoldo Paroni, is
the real imbecile. Then Luca leaves to shoot himself, keeping the
note in his jacket pocket where it will be found the next day.*

To Clothe the Naked (Vestire gli ignudi)

First production: Teatro Quirino, Rome, 14 Nov. 1922 (Maria Melato-
Annibale Betrone Company).
Revivals: Teatro Argentina, Rome, May 1925, followed by European
tour (Luigi Pirandello's Company); Teatro Quirino, Rome, 12 June
1943 (Paola Borboni's Company); as *Naked*, Royal Court Theatre,
London, 4 Apr. 1963 (trans. Diane Cilento; dir. David Williams; with
Diane Cilento); Teatro Valle Teatro Stabile di Roma, Apr. 1966 (dir.
Vito Pandolfi; with Adriana Asti).
First British production: Royalty Theatre, London, 18 Mar. 1927
(trans. Arthur Livingston; dir. Theodore Komisarjevsky).
First US production: Princess Theatre, New York, 8 Nov. 1926
(trans. Arthur Livingston).
Film version: 1953 (dir. Marcello Pagliero; with Eleonora Rossi-Drago).
First published: Maschere nude, Vol. VII (Florence: Bemporad, 1923).
Translations: as *Naked*, Arthur Livingston, in *Each in His Own Way
and Two Other Plays* (London: Dent, 1923); William Murray, *To
Clothe the Naked and Two Other Plays* (New York: Dutton, 1962).

*Ersilia Drei is recovering from a suicide attempt and has been
befriended by Lodovico Nota, an ageing writer. In the first act
he uses her life story as living subject matter for his own work,
and she goes along willingly with this. She had finally attempted
suicide after a series of disasters, beginning with the death of a*

51

child in her care, daughter of the Italian Consul in Smirne. She then had an unhappy love affair with Franco Laspiga, who left her for a woman from his own class, and after briefly turning to prostitution Ersilia finally attempted suicide. But Ersilia's tragic account of her life undergoes a transformation when she is put under pressure by a reporter, anxious to find out more details of her time at the Consul's house, and then when Franco Laspiga comes to try and make amends to her. He is convinced that she tried to kill herself for love of him, and tells her he has jilted his fiancee and is willing to marry her. Ersilia tries to put him off, telling him about her prostitution and denying that he has been the cause of her unhappiness. Then the Consul arrives, and a further twist is added to the story. Ersilia and the Consul had been lovers, and while they were together the child had fallen to her death from a balcony. The Consul begins by calling Ersilia a whore, but ends up admitting his own passionate need of her. Ersilia is driven to despair, because both men from her past insist on projecting their own versions of her life-story onto her, and she feels that she has no room to breathe. Finally she takes poison, and explains that all she had wanted from life was a decent garment with which to clothe her nakedness, a garment of respectability and love, both denied her in life. Ersilia finally dies with all her illusions stripped away, completely naked.

Marta Abba . . . profoundly impressed the house with the poignancy of her acting as the wretched Ersilia. Pathos and passion were alike at her command, and with them went a 'petitionary grace' which is peculiarly her own. Gina Graziosi was droll as a termagant landlady. The men, at least according to English standards . . . lacked distinction. And, as usual with these Italian companies, the prompter kept up a kind of hissing commentary on the play throughout the evening.

The Times, 23 June 1925

The Man with the Flower in His Mouth
(L'uomo dal fiore in bocca)

First production: Teatro Degli Indipendenti, Rome, 21 Feb. 1923
    (dir. Anton Bragaglia).

First British production: BBC Radio, 23 Feb. 1929 (trans. Arthur
Livingston); on 14 July 1930, a production by the BBC made this
the first play ever transmitted on British television.
First US production: Playhouse Repertory Company, New York,
10 July 1953 (trans. Arthur Livingston).
First published: as a short story, 'Caffé notturno', *La Rassegna Italiana*,
Rome, 15 Aug. 1918; as a play, in *Maschere nude*, Vol. XX,
(Florence: Bemporad, 1926).
Translations: Arthur Livingston, *The Dial*, New York, Oct. 1923, and
in *Pirandello's One-Act Plays* (New York: Dutton, 1928); William
Murray, *Pirandello's One-Act Plays* (New York: Doubleday, 1964);
Gigi Gatti and Terry Doyle, in Robert Rietti, ed., *Collected Plays*,
Vol. I (London: John Calder, 1987).

*Two men meet in a café. The Commuter has just missed his
train, and while he is waiting he strikes up a conversation with
The Man with the Flower in His Mouth. The man talks at
inordinate length about trivial things — the wrapping of a
parcel in a shop or the furnishings of doctors' waiting rooms —
but gradually reveals his obsessive interest in the minutiae of
daily life: he has a cancer growing in his mouth and, faced with
advancing death, he seizes every opportunity to observe life. His
fear of death has driven him to a point beyond human feelings,
and he even rejects his poor wife, who is forced to follow him
around, spying on him round corners. The Man has become
anarchic and irrational because life has lost its meaning for
him. All that remains, as the flower grows and spreads its
poison, are chance encounters in casual meeting places.*

The Life That I Gave You
(La vita che ti diedi)

First production: Teatro Quirino, Rome, 12 Oct. 1923 (Alda Borelli's
Company).
First British production: Little Theatre, London, 4 Oct. 1924 (trans.
Clifford Bax).
Revivals: Theatre Royal, Huddersfield, 11 May 1931 (trans. A. O.
Roberts); Civic Theatre, Leeds, 10 Sept. 1958 (trans. Frederick May).

First published: Maschere nude, Vol. VIII (Florence: Bemporad, 1924).
Translations: Frederick May, in E. Martin Browne, ed., *Three Plays* (Harmondsworth: Penguin, 1959).

The play opens with peasant women praying outside the room of Donn'Anna's only son, who has just died. Donn' Anna is distraught by her son's death, but when she finds a letter written by the dead man to the woman he loved, urging her to leave her husband and family and live with him, she decides to finish the letter and send it. By doing this she believes that she will in some way prolong her son's life through the woman he loved. When Lucia, the recipient of the letter, arrives, Donn'Anna is unable to admit that the man they both loved is dead. Lucia believes he has abandoned her and breaks down, telling Donn'Anna that she is pregnant. Donn'Anna is delighted; her son will stay alive in the new child. But in sending the letter to Lucia, Donn'Anna has also written to Lucia's mother, Francesca, and when Francesca arrives Donn'Anna is forced to confess that she has still not told Lucia the truth. Francesca is appalled, but before either mother can tell her, Lucia comes in and guesses what has happened. Lucia's grief is so great that it effectively destroys all Donn'Anna's illusions of her son still being alive somewhere in the mind. The lives of both older and younger woman have been destroyed.

The Other Son (L'altro figlio)

First production: in Tuscan dialect version by Ferdinando Paolieri, Teatro Nazionale, Rome, 23 Nov. 1923 (Raffaella and Garibalda Niccoli Company).
First British production: Questors' Theatre, London, 6 Feb. 1954 (trans. Frederick May; dir. Pamela Richards).
First published: as·a short story, in *La Lettura*, Feb. 1905; as a play, in *Maschere nude*, Vol. VIII, second edition (Milan: Mondadori, 1937).
Translations: as *The House with the Column*, Elizabeth Abbott, in *Pirandello's One-Act Plays* (New York: Dutton, 1928); William Murray, *Pirandello's One-Act Plays* (New York: Doubleday, 1964).

Maragrazia, a poor peasant woman, goes to the village letter-writer to ask him yet again to write to her sons in America. When a new young doctor arrives in the village he discovers that the letter-writer has been deceiving Maragrazia, taking her money and writing just a few scribbles on a page in return. The Doctor is horrified, but the neighbours are less sympathetic; they tell him she drove her sons away with her misery years ago, but that if she only wanted it, she could live in comfort and be loved by her remaining son, Rocco, who lives in the house with the column in the village. Rocco tells the Doctor that he always keeps a bed made up for his mother in his house, and in the fourteen years since the other boys left for America he has continued to provide for his mother. The Doctor is completely mystified, and asks Maragrazia to explain why she neglects the son who loves her and tries vainly to contact the ones who have abandoned her. Maragrazia tells her terrible story: years before she had been brutally raped by a bandit, one of a group who had not only murdered her husband but had played bowls with the heads of their victims. Left pregnant after the rape, she had hated the son from the moment of his conception, and had never been able to bring herself to touch him or even look at him. The Doctor asks how poor Rocco is to blame for this, and Maragrazia admits that he is completely innocent. The problem is that he is so like his father that he is a daily reminder of the horror of the past, and this is too great for her to overcome. The play ends with Maragrazia dictating yet another letter, this time with the help of the Doctor.

Each in His Own Way
(Ciascuno a suo modo)

First production: Teatro dei Filodrammatici, Milan, 22 May 1924 (Dario
    Niccodemi's Company; with Vera Vergani and Luigi Cimara).
Revivals: Teatro Stabile della Città di Genova, 12 Oct. 1961
    (dir. Luigi Squarzina).
First British productions: Nottingham University Drama Society,
    27 Feb 1952 (trans. G. H. William); BBC Third Programme,
    29 June 1952 (trans. Arthur Livingston).
First US production: 44th St. Theatre, New York, 1924 (trans.
    Arthur Livingston).
First published: Maschere nude, Vol. IX (Florence: Bemporad, 1924).

Translations: Arthur Livingston, *Each in His Own Way and Two Other
   Plays* (London: Dent, 1923); reprinted in Eric Bentley, ed., *Naked
   Masks* (New York: Dutton, 1952).

---

*The play is divided into four parts, two acts with a narrative
story line, and two choral intermezzi, in which groups of theatre
critics and members of the public debate what they have just
seen. The third act does not take place because of an
interruption by characters from the intermezzi. Donna Livia is
giving a party, and during the evening she interrogates one of
her guests, the cynical Diego Cinci, about her son, Doro. She is
convinced that he is in love with Delia Morello, a woman with a
scandalous reputation, whose former lover committed suicide.
Doro has publicly defended Delia Morello against the
accusations of Francesco, but when he arrives he says he is
willing to make peace and change his mind. Francesco arrives
and also decides to change his mind. At this point, Delia
Morello comes to thank Doro for defending her. Doro is
delighted, but then tells her the details of Francesco's counter
argument. At this, Delia agrees that the second version of events
might also be true. In the ensuing first intermezzo, Amalia
Moreno, an actress present in the audience, is outraged by what
she claims is a story about her and her lover, Nuti. The main
play continues with Doro and Francesco preparing to fight a
duel, despite being strongly discouraged by Diego Cinci, who
argues that truth is relative. Delia's lover, Michele, offers yet
another version of the story, but all discussion stops when Delia
and Michele come face to face and are overcome by their
passion for one another. In the second intermezzo Amalia
Moreno is so infuriated by what she has seen that she storms
backstage, and the play ends with accounts of how she has
slapped the Leading Lady who played Delia Morello, and the
play has had to be discontinued.*

I staged the 'world premiere' of the play — it was originally given, I
believe, in 1925, the only production until mine. There are speeches like,
'Pirandello is on the stage', 'he's left', 'he's run away', etc., which made
the 'premiere' setting inevitable. By accentuating the costumes, I was
able to contrast a certain reality — the Italian stage of the 'twenties and,

implicitly, the stage of any theatre, any time and everywhere — with the reactions of an urban audience, a multifarious collectivity, barely kept together by the fact that at that time any audience was almost completely a bourgeois audience. . . .

The actor who played, let's say, Diego Cinci, was in fact asked to play three roles: the character Diego Cinci in the play within the play, the actor who played Diego Cinci, and the actor of the Repertory Theatre of Genoa, Alberto Lionello, who presented those two other levels. Thanks to the actor's skill and the dynamics of his relations to the other actors, I was able to show this one piece of reality in its three contradictory facets.

At the end of the first act I had the curtain fall as if it were time for the intermission. I also had the applause and booing recorded as if it were a performance of Pirandello's time, with the typical reactions of his premieres. When the curtain re-opened almost instantly, the setting showed the foyer of the theatre with people talking and arguing as if coming from boxes and galleries. Curtain again, and when it re-opened there was the second act of the play. Curtains closed and re-opened, and then the setting showed the circular corridor along the boxes, with people listening both to the uproar coming from the orchestra and to a brawl that had started on stage. I thought I found the touchstone of my production precisely at this point. I had the mass of spectators rush through the door leading to the stage, occupying it like an army of invaders. The stage was being blasphemed and desecrated — and, therefore, it too was denounced as a part of reality rather than as a temple devoted to some mysterious ritual.

Luigi Squarzina, 'Directing Pirandello Today',
in Glauco Cambon, ed., *Pirandello: a Collection of Critical Essays*
(Prentice-Hall, 1967)

The Festival of Our Lord of the Ship
(La sagra del signore della nave)

One-act play for a large cast.
First production: Teatro Odescalchi, Rome, 4 Apr. 1925 (Teatro d'Arte Company, dir. Luigi Pirandello).
Revivals: Palermo, Aug. 1951 (special production by Tatiana Pawlova); Teatro di Verdura nel Parco della Villa Castelnuovo, Palermo, 5 Aug. 1967 (dir. Maurizio Scaparro).
First published: Il convegno, Milan, 30 Sept. 1924; also in *Maschere nude*, Vol. XII (Florence: Bemporad, 1925).

Translations: as *Our Lord of the Ship*, Blanche Valentine Mitchell, in
   Pirandello's One-Act Plays (New York: Dutton, 1928); William
   Murray, *Pirandello's One-Act Plays* (New York: Doubleday, 1964).

---

*This play is set in a village where a statue of Christ has saved
many sailors from shipwreck. The action takes place during a
festival in honour of this image, and the peasants eat and drink
to excess as they celebrate. A young schoolteacher is disgusted
by the gross behaviour of the villagers, and cannot understand
how a religious event can provide the occasion for such
bestiality, but he clings to the idea of the inherent nobility of
mankind. The father of one of his pupils, Signor Lavaccara, has
raised an enormous pig of which he has become fond, but allows
it to be slaughtered nevertheless. The killing of the pigs takes
place off-stage, but the screams of the dying animals can be
heard clearly. The Schoolteacher is forced by Signor Lavaccara
to admit that the sounds made by the pigs and the noise made by
humans are indistinguishable, and the schoolteacher's idealism
collapses. The play ends with a procession, 'the great macabre ,
blood-soaked Crucifix' being carried through the throng, and
Signor Lavaccara pointing out the terrible irony of the bestial,
butchering peasants who are dissolving into tears at the sight of
the cross.*

In this one-act play, the brutish nature of crowds was given a full treat-
ment: a greedy, loud-mouthed, festive and sceptical crowd that grabs at
the first symbol that speaks of some kind of mystery that we all harbour
within us. In this work the animal nature of human beings finds a com-
forting portrayal both in its brutality and in its aspiration towards
something higher and divine. It is only a matter of degree. . . .

   The two plays chosen for the opening night of the Teatro d'Arte are
among the most choreographic and visual available. With these two
plays the theatre is able to manifest all its resources and possibilities.
Footlights have been abolished. Lighting is effected by means of a series
of spots in five colours, placed both front of house and on stage. These
spots plunge the stage into pools of colour. With careful control amazing
effects of proximity and distance can be obtained. The actors are not
highlighted by a shadowless light, like little figures under a stereoscope,
but immersed in a warm and general light that can change tone by
minute and imperceptible degrees. Provided that it is not abused, this

method of lighting could be used to compensate for shallow but wide stages like the one at the Teatro Valle. The setting is created emblematically. A large piece of cloth, called a cyclorama, covers the three walls of the stage. Against this, lit by spots of different tonal colours, are placed a few pieces of scenery so as to create the characters of the setting. This is a method adopted by art theatres abroad. Purple and grey are the informing colours of the whole auditorium, which is raked towards the stage and accommodates three blocks of grey seats on grey carpet; above a dress circle six rows deep in silver. A grey curtain with silver edges opens on to the purple carpet of the stage. The walls covered in grey material are lit by baroque lamps, and indeed the whole design of the theatre by Virgilio Marchi could be called baroque. The silver of the decorations, the mother-of-pearl and dove-coloured grey of the wall hangings and velvets, give a soft tone to the whole theatre. The golden heads of the ladies in the stalls seemed set in an antique jewel case.

The lamps cast a prism of light on the grey wall hangings. In the auditorium there is a lyrical quality that is even better discovered on going out into the foyer. There, windows, lamps, gratings, blinds form an orchestra of silver, emphasized by the brick yellow of the plaster and by the gleaming muted red of the curtains. The design of the whole theatre, with its system of levels, loggias, balconies, has a musical movement.

Corrado Alvaro, *Il Risorgimento*, 3 Apr. 1925, reprinted in
Alfredo Barbina, ed., *Cronache e scritti teatrali di Corrado Alvaro*
(Rome, 1976)

Diana and Tuda
(Diana e la Tuda)

First production: Schauspielhaus, Zurich, 20 Nov. 1926 (German
version by Hans Feist; dir. Richard Rosenheim).
First Italian production: Teatro Eden, Milan, 14 Jan. 1927 (Luigi
Pirandello's Company; with Marta Abba).
First published: Maschere nude, Vol. XXI (Florence: Bemporad, 1927).
Translation: as *Diana and Tuda*, Marta Abba (New York: Samuel
French, 1960).

Sirio Dossi is a sculptor, who is working on his ideal piece, a statue of Diana. He has decided that when he finishes it he will kill himself, because nothing else in life can compare with this work. His model is the beautiful, vivacious Tuda, who is strongly attracted to him. Sirio is so devoted to his work and so jealous of it, that he does not want Tuda to model for anyone else. He offers her a compromise: if she will marry him and agree to model only for him, he will give her security, all the money she needs, and complete freedom to live her own life. Sirio already has a mistress, Sara, and Tuda is loved by Giuncano, an older man who is also a sculptor, but whom she does not love in return. Tuda agrees to this strange marriage, and at first amuses herself by spending large sums of Sirio's money, but when Sara taunts her with her promises of fidelity to a man who does not love her and merely pays her bills, she decides to declare her independence by going to model for his arch-rival, Caravani. After Tuda has gone, Sara confesses her own unhappiness to Giuncano, who is also suffering from unrequited love. Tuda returns, a harder person without her previous exuberance, and declares that she has realized that she needs Sirio's art in order to live forever. She urges Sirio to take what remains of her life and put it into his statue, but when she goes to embrace the statue, Sirio intervenes, and Giuncano, in a moment of blind rage, stabs him. The play ends with Tuda acknowledging that now Sirio is dead the great work that would have immortalized her will never be finished and she is reduced to nothing.

The Wives' Friend
(L'amica delle mogli)

First production: Teatro Argentina, Rome, 28 Apr. 1927 (Luigi Pirandello's Company; with Marta Abba).
Revivals: Teatro Quirino, Rome, 1943 (Pirandellian Company; with Paola Borboni); Teatro Carignano, Turin, Oct. 1968 (De Lullo-Falck-Valli-Albani Company; dir. Giorgio De Lullo).
First published: Maschere nude, Vol. XXII (Florence: Bemporad, 1927).
Translation: Marta Abba (New York: Samuel French, 1959).

Marta Tolosani has been the friend of a lot of people, men and women, who have all managed to get married. Only she has remained single, and once the marriages have taken place she has become the friend of all the wives. But when one of the couples, Fausto and Elena, come back from their honeymoon, one of Marta's friends, Francesco, understands that she might have married him if he had offered, and is deeply suspicious of Marta's closeness to Fausto. He puts doubts into Elena's mind, although Elena is ill and eventually dies. Marta rejects Francesco's advances because she cannot contemplate an adulterous relationship, and he is so appalled by the prospect of Fausto now being free and able to marry Marta himself that he kills Fausto and announces that he had committed suicide because of his grief at Elena's death. But Marta understands what has happened, and so Francesco loses whatever faint chance he might still have had of keeping her respect and winning her love.

Bellavita

First production: Teatro Eden, Milan, 27 May 1927 (Almirante-Rissone-Tofano Company).
First British production: Studio Theatre Club at Mahatma Ghandi Assembly Hall, London, 22 Jan. 1956.
First published: Il Secolo, XX, Milan, July 1928; also in *Maschere nude*, Vol. VIII, second edition (Milan: Mondadori, 1937).
Translation: William Murray, *Pirandello's One-Act Plays* (New York: Doubleday, 1964).

The notary, Denora, goes to see his lawyer, Contento, in a state of great agitation. Mrs. Contento tries to calm him, but in vain. A story emerges of a son, born to a woman who has died, and who may or may not be Denora's own child. Denora had been having an affair with the dead woman, and her husband, Bellavita, instead of being openly jealous and hostile, has been so utterly charming and respectful to Denora that it is driving him mad, because he feels that he is unable properly to express his grief. Bellavita even came to tell Denora he had ordered two wreaths for the funeral, one for each of them. Then Bellavita, a thin, shabby man in deep mourning, arrives, and Contento sends Denora out of the room while he tries to reason with him. He offers Bellavita Denora's suggestion of sending the boy away to the best boarding school in Naples, but Bellavita refuses. He also refuses to stop being publicly respectful of Denora, because in this way, by making Denora seem ridiculous, he is able to exact his revenge. Denora rushes in, furious, and Bellavita immediately starts smiling and bowing. This, he claims, is the best way for wronged husbands to behave, because in this way they can make the lover look a fool. He suggests that Giorgino, one of the clients in the waiting room, might do well to follow his example, and the play ends with him rushing out after Denora to continue his plan of public humiliation by exaggerated friendliness amid gales of laughter.

Scamandro

First production: Teatro dell'Academia dei Fidenti, Florence, 19 Feb. 1928 (Gruppo Academico; with music by Fernando Liuzzi.)
Unpublished, and not translated into English.

The New Colony (La nuova colonia)

First production: Teatro Argentina, Rome, 24 Mar. 1928 (Luigi Pirandello's Company; with Marta Abba and Lamberto Picasso).
Revivals: Teatro delle Arte, Rome, 5 Jan. 1940 (dir. Anton Giulio Bragaglia); Teatro Stabile, Naples, 8 Apr. 1958 (dir. Vittorio Viviani; with Marta Abba).
First US production: reading at Studio Schubert, Chicago, 1931 (trans. Samuel Putnam).
First published: Maschere nude, Vol. XXIII (Florence: Bemporad, 1928).
Translation: Marta Abba, *The Mountain Giants and Other Plays* (New York: Crown, 1958).

The action takes place in Nuccio's tavern, where Padron Nocio, the local landowner, accuses Tobba, an old fisherman, of putting crazy ideas in the head of his son, Doro, about an island where the evils of this world can be avoided. The one good character is La Spera, a prostitute, whose lover, Currao, is another fisherman, and like many of the others he ekes out his wretched pay with smuggling. La Spera wants to escape from the degraded lives they all lead, and she urges them to go to the island, despite stories that the island is destined one day to sink under the sea. The smugglers and La Spera go to the island, a former penal colony that had been abandoned because of the encroaching water, but to the poverty-stricken group from the mainland it seems like a place of hope, and they plan to create a new society. La Spera tells the others that a miracle has occurred: she is able to breast-feed her baby son, something that had previously been impossible for her. Tobba tells the others that this is truly a sign from God and all kneel in prayer. But the promises of new life are not fulfilled, and quarrels break out because La Spera is the only woman on the island and all the men want to possess her. Then Padron Nocio comes across to the island, bringing his daughter Mita and some other women with him, and does a deal with Currao to take over control of the colony. La Spera becomes increasingly isolated, as Currao proposes to marry Mita and tries to take away La Spera's baby. In the final moments of the play, La Spera is treated as a whore by the others, who urge Currao to snatch the child out of her arms. La Spera cries out that if he does so, the earth will quake, and so great is the strength of her goodness that the island is swallowed up by a tidal wave, and in the total destruction of the new order only La Spera and her baby remain alive.

The New Colony is the least melancholic of all Pirandello's plays, in fact it is the most hopeful of all his works.

The production deserves full praise for its structuring, for the order in the apparent chaos, for the perfection of every detail. Last night at the Manzoni Theatre the company demonstrated their first-class sense of cohesion, discipline and passion.

Each one of the actors deserves a mention, even those in the smallest parts, for nobody was less than excellent. It will suffice to note that through her dramatic strength, and, above all, for the clear, gentle sweetness in her lyrical scenes of goodness, Marta Abba deserved the whole-hearted praise of the audience, and Picasso performed with a solemn, intense and quite remarkable strength.

Renato Simoni, *Il Corriere della Sera*, Milan, 19 Apr. 1928

Either Somebody's or Nobody's
(O di uno o di nessuno)

First production: Teatro di Torino, Turin, 4 Nov. 1929 (Almirante-Rissone-Tofano Company; with Vittorio De Sica).
Revivals: Teatro Eliseo, Rome, 29 Sept. 1940 (Daniela Palmer Company); Teatro Stabile, Palermo, Jan. 1957 (dir. Lucio Chiaravelli).
First published: Maschere nude, Vol. XXV (Florence: Bemporad, 1929).
Translation: Frederick May, unpublished.

Two close friends, Carlino and Tito, have the same mistress, Melina, a woman whom they have set up in an apartment in the suburbs where they visit on alternate days. They are all content with this situation, until Melina discovers that she is pregnant and does not know which of the two men is the father. Carlino and Tito quarrel violently, and decide finally either to abandon Melina or to force her to give away the child and carry on living as they had all done before. But Melina refuses; they may be uncertain who the father is, but she is quite sure that she is the mother. The two men abandon her, and she dies giving birth to the child. Carlino and Tito are now overcome with remorse and both offer to take the child, but Merletti, another typically Pirandellian rationalist figure, points out that he cannot act as Solomon did when confronted with two mothers claiming the same infant. Melina's deathbed scene, which runs throughout the third act, is one of Pirandello's most extended tear-jerking sequences. The dilemma facing the two men is resolved by a deus ex machina. Signor Franzoni, Melina's next door neighbour, has had to chose between his wife and baby when her labour went wrong. He chose to save his wife, and the baby died. Merletti proposes that Melina's baby should be given to the Franzonis to be brought up in the place of their own dead child, and so Carlino and Tito are finally able to forgive one another and become friends again, while the baby goes to two parents who will love him as their own son.

Lazarus (Lazzaro)

First production: as *Though One Rose*, Theatre Royal, Huddersfield,
8 July 1929 (Hull Repertory Theatre Company; trans. C. K. Scott-
Moncrieff; dir. Arthur Whatmore).
First Italian production: Teatro di Torino, Turin, 9 July 1929 (Marta
Abba's Company).
Revivals: Teatro Odeon, Milan, 16 Apr. 1952 (Andreina Pagnini's
Company; dir. Claudio Fino; with Giorgio De Lullo); Compagnia del
Dramma Italiana, 1966-69 (with Ennio Balbo and Lea Padovani).
First published: Maschere nude, Vol. XXVI (Florence: Bemporad,
1930).
Translation: Frederick May, in E. Martin Browne, ed., *Three Plays*
(Harmondsworth: Penguin, 1959); reprinted in Robert Rietti, ed.,
Collected Plays, Vol. I (London: John Calder, 1987).
First US production: Henry Sloane Coffin Building, New York,
2 Apr. 1963 (trans. Frederick May).

*Diego Spina, a wealthy man with rigid, puritanical standards of
behaviour, has long since driven away his wife, Sara. Since Sara
left, Diego has denied her access to her two children, Lucio and
Lia, and Sara has fallen in love with Arcadipane, a peasant
farmer, and has given up her middle-class life in order to live
with him and with their children out in the country. Left behind
with their father, Lucio and Lia have become withdrawn and
repressed, Lia living at home and Lucio studying to be a priest.
Lia's pet rabbit dies, and Dr. Gionni claims to have restored it to
life with an injection. Diego refuses to accept this irrational
notion, but then irrationality is forced upon him when Sara
arrives to tell him that Lucio has decided to abandon the
priesthood and is staying with her. Diego is appalled by this
news and by the fact that Sara has dared to enter his house after
so many years, but Sara tells him that Lucio has come back to
her to be reborn through his lost mother's love. Diego is overwhelmed by emotion and runs out of the house, where he is hit
by a car and declared dead. The second act takes place in Sara's
idyllic country home, where Sara and Lucio are rediscovering
one another, and news is brought there that Diego has also been
resurrected by Dr. Gionni's injection. Diego's death causes him
to lose his faith in God completely: death for him was just*

nothingness, but it is precisely this that leads Lucio to make a declaration of faith and commit himself again to the priesthood. Diego, however, has unleashed all his pent-up feelings, and tries to kill Arcadipane. Lucio confronts him, and the tables are turned as the self-righteous father and doubting son become a man without faith and a devoutly believing priest. Lucio forces Diego to see the damage his past unforgiveness has caused and Diego asks him for help. Lucio tells him to think of resurrection, and Diego is able to let Lia go to live with her mother. The play ends with the statement that a true miracle has taken place.

The play suffers both in texture and in structure from having too many threads; but it remains nevertheless a notable essay in abstinence. There are few fireworks, and very little of the old tortuosity of thought. The puppets have become almost human personifications of frailties and failings in a modern 'mystery' and the central figure of the mother is a fine creation of sincerity to which the whole play is attuned.

Manchester Guardian, 9 July 1929

As You Desire Me (Come tu mi vuoi)

First production: Teatro dei Filodrammatici, Milan, 18 Feb. 1930 (Marta Abba's Company).

Revivals: Teatro Eliseo, Rome, 26 Oct. 1940 (Evi Maltagliati's Company); Teatro Quirino, Rome, 20 June 1943 (Paola Borboni's Company); Teatro Quirino, Rome, 21 Mar. 1953 (Marta Abba's Company); Teatro Eliseo, Rome, Oct. 1966 (Anna Proclemer and Giorgio Albertazzi's Company; dir. Giorgio Albertazzi); Teatro Stabile della Città di Torino, Turin, 1980 (dir. Susan Sonntag).

First British production: Royalty Theatre, London, 1 Oct. 1934 (trans. Andree Zaro; dir. Peter Godfrey).

First US production: Elliott Theatre, New York, 28 Jan. 1931 (adapted by Dimitri Ostrow).

Film versions: Metro Goldwyn Mayer, Hollywood, 1932 (dir. George Fitzmaurice; with Greta Garbo and Erich Von Stroheim); as *Asi Te Deseo*, Orion, Montevideo, 1947 (dir.Belisario Garcia Villar).

First published: Maschere nude, Vol. XXVIII (Florence: Bemporad, 1930).

Translation: Samuel Putnam (New York: Dutton, 1931); Marta Abba (New York: Samuel French, 1959).

The action takes place ten years after the First World War, and is set in Berlin and Udine. Carl Salter, a wealthy German writer, lives with his sexually ambiguous daughter, Mop, and his mistress, the Unknown Woman. The opening sequence sets the tone of decadence that prevails throughout: Mop is sitting crying, when Salter rushes in carrying a revolver, and then the Unknown Woman appears, followed by a crowd of drunken young men all trying to seduce her. Both Salter and Mop are in love with the Unknown Woman, but she is contemptuous of both of them. Into this milieu comes Boffi, on behalf of his friend in Udine, Bruno. Bruno's villa was broken into ten years earlier, his wife Cia was raped and carried off, and Bruno has become convinced that the Unknown Woman is his lost Cia. Boffi tells her this story, and she hears him out without comment, except to note that if Bruno believes he can find his wife of ten years earlier unchanged then he must be mad. She agrees to go to Udine, and Salter tries to kill himself but fails. Once in Udine, the Unknown Woman is scrutinized by Zio Salesio and Zia Lena who are trying to verify whether she is in fact the lost bride. The Unknown Woman is troubled by the doubts cast upon her identity in this new world, and points out that even Bruno is not entirely convinced, however much he might want to be, because they all require concrete proof rather than faith. Meanwhile, Salter claims to have found the real Cia in a mental hospital in Vienna, and brings her to the villa to confront the Unknown Woman. Faced with two possible Cias, Bruno inclines towards the mad woman, but then the Unknown Woman gives such a graphic account of Cia's story that everyone comes to believe that she is indeed the real Cia. But it is too late; the Unknown Woman had asked for faith and love and not received it. As the play ends, Cia leaves the villa forever, returning to her life in Berlin with Salter, and the mad woman helplessly repeats the only word she knows while the family stand around appalled.

Tonight We Improvise
(Questa sera si recita a soggetto)

First production: as *Heute Abend Wird aus dem Stegreif Gespielt,*

Neues Schauspielhaus, Koenigsberg, 25 Jan. 1930 (German version by Harry Kahn).

First Italian production: Teatro di Torino, Turin, 14 Apr. 1930 (dir. Guido Salvini.

Revivals: Piccolo Teatro di Milano, 19 Nov. 1949 (dir. Giorgio Strehler); Teatro delle Arti, Rome, 15 Mar. 1957 (Compagnia del Teatro Italiano; dir. Guido Salvini); Teatro Quirino, Rome, 1961-62 (adapted by Vittorio Gassman and G. Guerriere; Compagnia del Teatro Popolare Italiano; dir. Vittorio Gassman), Teatro Quirino, Rome, 21 Mar. 1968 (Compagnia del Dramma Italiano; dir. Paolo Ciurranna).

First British production: Riley Smith Theatre, Leeds, 29 Nov. 1955 (trans. Frederick May).

First published: Maschere nude, Vol. XXVII (Florence: Bemporad, 1930).

Translation: as *Tonight We Improvise,* Samuel Putnam (New York: Dutton, 1932); Marta Abba (New York: Samuel French, 1960); J. Douglas Campbell and Leonard Sbrocchi (Ottawa: Canadian Society for Italian Studies, 1987).

The action of the play moves around the theatre, between stage and auditorium. A director, Hinkfuss, is trying to create a play with a group of actors. He wants them to improvise, without a script, but the actors are unhappy with this idea. Hinkfuss devises some coups de théâtre — *a Sicilian religious procession, an airfield with planes — and the actors constantly revolt against his tyrannical directorial style, which seeks show and no substance. The story line that Hinkfuss has chosen for his actors concerns Signora Ignazia and her four daughters, Mommina, Totina, Dorina and Nene. Signora Ignazia, a Neapolitan transposed to Sicily, has brought up her girls in a way that is regarded as too loose for the village, and she particularly dislikes Mommina's young man, Rico Verri, an airforce officer, who is very straightlaced. When Sampognetta, her husband, played by the Old Comic Actor, one of the chief rebels against the director, is killed off in a fight, the women have to fend for themselves, which they do very well. Totina becomes a famous singer and keeps her mother and two of her sisters in luxury, though Mommina has married Verri instead. Verri is so jealous that he keeps her locked inside her own home, and when Mommina learns that her mother and sisters have come back to the village with a production of* Il Trovatore, *she tries in her prison to tell her little children about theatre. The effort is so great that she falls dead, and when her relatives arrive they are too late. Hinkfuss is so pleased with this piece of improvisation that he breaks the spell by commenting on it, and as the Leading Lady playing Mommina comes round slowly from this traumatic piece of work, Hinkfuss ends the play with yet another of his pompous pronouncements on the requirements of theatre.*

In Koenigsberg *Tonight We Improvise* was a clear and total success, and was played in an honest, full version. This was not the case in Berlin. The play was given to a director whose name is best forgotten despite his fame, and was flaccid, messy and incoherent. The director was incapable of working with the dramatic impulse of the piece, or with its satirical force. The picturesque elements became forced and obtrusive, as in the kind of print where the colour has spilled over the outlines of the drawing. In short, it was a fiasco, and a noisy, unpleasant one because, apart from the stupid direction and the unfocused acting, there was a group of scoundrelly henchmen from the Reinhardt faction who, rightly or wrongly, thought they could see characteristics of their master in Pirandello's caricature of a director.

Pirandello suffered all the humiliations of a newcomer for that insult; and he was indeed a newcomer in the field of disasters, but what offended him most was the savage fury directed against his concept of theatre which he had set out in *Tonight We Improvise.*

Pietro Solari, 'Giornate a Berlino',
in *Almanacco Letterario Bompiani* (1938)

Finding Oneself (Trovarsi)

First production: Teatro dei Fiorenti, Naples, 4 Nov. 1932 (Almirante-
    Rissone-Tofano Company).
First British production: as *A Woman in Search of Herself,*
    BBC Radio 3, 30 June 1987 (trans. Susan Bassnett and David Hirst).
First published: Maschere nude, Vol. XXIX (Milan: Mondadori, 1932).
Translation: as *To Find Oneself,* Marta Abba (New York: Samuel
    French, 1959).

A group of people are gathered at the seaside house of Elisa, a wealthy socialite, to meet her friend, the famous actress, Donata Genzi. Rumours abound about Donata Genzi, but she appears to live so completely in her art that she is above passion. When Donata appears, she is distressed by the way in which Elisa's friends talk about her, confusing the woman and the actress and making the two indistinguishable. One of the guests, Count Mola, has a young nephew, Eli Nielsen, whose mother and Swedish seafaring father are both dead. Count Mola insists that Eli must come to Elisa's house, to prevent him going out in his boat in a storm. Eli refuses to go to dinner with the other guests, and, while he is waiting, Donata, who has retired to her room, comes down again and meets him. In a rash moment she and Eli go off in the boat together. The boat sinks, and Eli manages to save Donata who, it seems, has wanted to die. As he nurses her back to health they fall in love, and for the first time she feels real passion. Eli asks her to marry him and she agrees, but he also wants her to give up the theatre, which she is reluctant to do. In the third act, Eli storms into the hotel suite he is sharing with Donata and tells Count Mola that he is leaving Donata and going back to the sea. He cannot bear to watch her on stage, seeing all their intimacy exposed to other people's gaze. Count Mola tells him that Donata's performance has been truly dreadful, and that Eli's presence in the theatre has prevented her from acting her best. But then, after Eli leaves, Elisa and Donata come back with news of the triumphal success of the evening. Donata realizes that she cannot have Eli and her life as an actress, and in the solitude of her hotel room she conjures up characters from the play in which she has been performing that evening, reliving her success and admitting her loneliness. As the play ends, Donata is alone on stage, reflecting that one can only find oneself in the act of creating, because nothing else is really true.

Last Tuesday's play translation by Susan Bassnett and David Hirst went a very long way towards freeing Pirandello from his English shackles of the past. The dialogue was springy and subtle, suggesting, though not mimicking, authentic speech.

This gave the ideas and images quite unfamiliar and very welcome vitality. They no longer sounded unappealing, not to say incredible, as accounts of personal experience; so that when a famous actress, Donata Genzi (played by Gemma Jones), tries to discover who she is — if anyone — outside the roles she plays, we share what she is doing.

The Times, 7 July 1987

When One Is Somebody
(Quando si è qualcuno)

First production: in a Spanish version by Homer Guglielmini, entitled
  Cuando Si Es Alguien, Teatro Odeon, Buenos Aires, 20 Sept. 1933.
First Italian production: Teatro del Casino Municipale, San Remo,
  7 Nov. 1933 (Marta Abba's Company; dir. Marta Abba).
First published: Maschere nude, Vol. XXX (Milan: Mondadori, 1933).
Translation: as *When Someone is Somebody*, Marta Abba, in *The
  Mountain Giants and Other Plays* (New York: Crown, 1958).

The nameless protagonist *** is an internationally famous writer, but his fame has become a kind of prison and he feels forced to write in accordance with the expectations of the world. He has fallen in love with a young woman, Veroccia, and has been writing exciting, passionate poetry, quite unlike his usual work, which he has published under the pseudonym Delago. In Act One, a group of young admirers of Delago hail him as the poet of hopefulness, the new writer for a new age. *** is happy with Veroccia who makes him feel young and full of energy, but when his predatory family arrive, to persuade him to accept a prestigious literary award, he gives in to them. He tells Veroccia he must give her up, and must also give up the mask of Delago, the youthful poet, because he will shortly be exposed as a fraud anyway. In Act Two, *** is in his study, amid dusty images of great Italian writers of the past, and when Veroccia comes with her sister and brother-in-law to attack him for his moral cowardice, *** is so far back inside his closed world that he cannot speak. The act ends with ***'s monologue on the sterility of fame and the loss of identity that it brings with it. In the third act, the party to honour *** is underway off-stage. Veroccia is prevented from going in and she cries out that *** is as good as dead already. The young people make one last attempt to *persuade *** to escape with them, but he refuses and the play ends with a set-piece, as *** is gradually turned into a statue of himself, alone and in the silence of lost hopes.*

The Changeling
(La favola del figlio cambiato)

First production: in a German version by Hans Redlich, entitled *Die Legende von Vertauschten Sohn*, Landtheater, Braunschweig, 13 Jan. 1934.

First Italian production: Teatro Reale dell'Opera, Rome, 24 Mar. 1934 (music by Gian Francesco Malipiero; conducted by Gino Marinuzzi; with Florica Christodoforeanu and Alessio De Paolis).

First Italian production without music: Teatro Piccinni, Piccolo Teatro della Città di Bari, 27 June 1949.

Revival: Piccolo Teatro della Città di Milano, 26 May 1957 (dir. Paolo Grassi and Giorgio Grassi).

First published: Milan: Ricordi, 1933; also in *Maschere nude*, Vol. X, second edition (Milan: Mondadori, 1938).

A poor peasant woman, the Mother, has her beautiful blond child stolen away in the night and replaced by a dark ugly baby. In her grief, she goes to the sorceress, Vanna Scoma, to ask if she has news. Vanna Scoma tells her to endure the loss, because it is in the child's best interest. He has been taken to be the child of a king, and will grow up with all material advantages. The suffering mother is heartbroken, but realizes that she is power-less to do anything. Years pass, and the dark baby grows up into the village idiot, cheerful but hopelessly afflicted. One day, a young prince comes to convalesce in the warmth of the southern sun. He is blond and handsome, but is ill and frail. The Mother and the Prince meet, and she tells him her story, convinced that he is her lost child. News comes that the king has died and the Prince must go back and take up the responsibilities of the kingdom. But he has discovered the love of his mother and the beauty of being poor yet free in a warm land. Refusing to go back, he accepts the version of events told by the Mother and the whole village, and sends the Idiot Boy back to become king.

Malipiero's new opera *The Changeling*, with the libretto by Pirandello, has been played in several German cities during the past few days. In the cities of Braunschweig and Darmstadt the opera was very well-received by the large numbers of select spectators. Chancellor Hitler was present at one performance. Therefore the Italian literary and cultural world was stunned when two days ago it was announced in Berlin that the Minister of Culture, on the advice of critics and members of the public, had decided to ban all subsequent performances of *The Changeling* because it was 'subversive and contrary to the interests of the German people's state'.

> Luigi Chiarini, 'Why Was *The Changeling* Banned in Germany?',
> *Quadrivio*, 18 Mar. 1934

The evening was not a pleasant one. The storm was already on its way at the end of the first act.

The singers took four curtain calls. Malipiero did not appear on the stage. Pirandello followed the progress of the disastrous performance from a side box in the second row.

> Matteo Intagliati, *Il Messagero*, Rome, 25 Mar. 1934

You Don't Know How
(Non si sa come)

First production: in a Czech version by Wenceslas Jirina, entitled
   Clovek Ani Nevi Jak, National Theatre, Prague, 19 Dec. 1934.
First Italian production: Teatro Argentina, Rome, 13 Dec. 1935
   (Ruggero Ruggeri's Company).
Revivals: Teatro Quirino, Rome, 10 Feb. 1946 (Memmo Benassi-Diana
   Torrieri's Company); Teatro Stabile, Genoa, 1966-67 (dir. Ivo Chisa
   and Luigi Squarzina).
First published: Maschere nude, Vol. XXXI (Milan: Mondadori, 1935).
Translation: as *No One Knows How,* Marta Abba (New York: Samuel
   French, 1961).

Romeo Daddi and his wife Bice are good friends with a naval officer, Giorgio, and his wife Ginevra. One day, while Giorgio was away, Romeo and Ginevra had a sudden instance of passion for each other, but nothing further came of it and Ginevra has all but forgotten it. Romeo, however, is tormented not by the fact itself, which is slight, but by the enormity of the way in which appearances can conceal. When the play opens the others talk about him as if he were mad, because he has suddenly become pathologically jealous of Bice, a woman whom everyone regards as the perfect wife. He is so obsessed with his own feelings of guilt that he seeks some kind of proof in Bice of a similar secret. He confesses that years ago he actually committed a murder, and has never been found out, and now he is tormented by the thought that the woman he loves might also have some dark thing to hide. Bice at first resists all his accusations, but then her suspicions are aroused that he might be having an affair with Ginevra. Romeo plays his trump card — he suggests that everyone, even the most innocent, might be capable of being unfaithful in dreams or thoughts, and then sees that this is indeed the case with Bice. Having discovered that she too has been unfaithful to him in her mind, he confesses his moment of passion with Ginevra to Giorgio, who shoots him. As he dies, Romeo utters the last words of the play — 'This, too, is only human'.

A Dream, But Perhaps It Isn't
(Sogno, ma forse no)

First production: in a Portuguese version by Abreu Beirao, entitled *Sonho (Ma Talvez Nao)*, National Theatre, Lisbon, 22 Sept. 1931.

First Italian production: Italian Radio, 11 Jan. 1936; Giardino d'Italia (student group from the University of Genoa), 10 Dec. 1937.

First published: La Lettura, Milan, Oct. 1929; also in *Maschere nude*, Vol. VI, second edition (Milan: Mondadori, 1936).

Translation: as *Dream, But Perhaps Not*, Samuel Putnam, in *This Quarter* (USA), June 1930; as *A Dream (and Perhaps It Isn't)*, Frederick May, in *Stand*, Vol. V, No. 3; William Murray, *Pirandello's One-Act Plays* (New York: Doubleday, 1964).

First British production: YWCA, Leeds, 18 Nov. 1955 (trans. Frederick May).

A Young Woman is dreaming, and the figure of her lover materializes in the room as a nightmare image. The Young

Woman and the Man relive their story, and his jealousy, together with her desire to have an expensive gift of a pearl necklace, lead to a moment of crisis, when he starts to strangle her because he knows that her former lover, who has been abroad, has come back and she is still in love with him. The Young Woman wakes up from the terrible dream, and immediately there is a knock at the door and a servant brings her a gift. It is the pearl necklace, and it has been sent by her former lover. There is a second knock and she hastily hides the necklace. This time, it is the Man from her dream, who has come to say how sorry he is that he was not able to buy the necklace for her because it had already been sold when he went to the shop. The play ends with the Young Woman feigning innocence and pouring out tea for both of them as the Man shows his jealousy and tells her that her former lover has come back from abroad. The dialogue is so close to the dialogue in the dream that the line between the two is blurred completely.

The Mountain Giants
(I giganti della montagna)

First production: Boboli Gardens, Florence, 5 June 1937 (dir. Renato Simoni).

Revivals: Piccolo Teatro della Città di Milano, 18 Oct. 1947 (dir. Paolo Grassi and Giorgio Strehler); Teatro Lirico, Milan, Nov. 1967 (dir. Giorgio Strehler).

First published: Act I, entitled *The Phantoms (I fantasmi)*, in *Quadrante*, Rome, 16 Dec. 1931; Act II, in *Nuova antologia*, Rome, Nov. 1932; also in *Maschere nude*, Vol. X, second edition (Milan: Mondadori, 1938).

Translation: Marta Abba, *The Mountain Giants and Other Plays* (New York: Crown, 1958).

The action of this unfinished play takes place in the fantastic Villa Scalogna, inhabited by a grotesque group of people led by Cotrone, a wizard and illusionist. Into this group come a company of travelling actors, driven on by Ilse, the leading lady, who is trying to make known the work of a young writer who killed himself for love of her. The title of the work is The Changeling, *and when the actors begin to perform it, it is in fact Pirandello's own play of the same name. Cotrone proposes to the company that they perform their play for the wedding festivities of the Mountain Giants, the strange unseen beings who inhabit the place. A makeshift stage is rigged up with a curtain round a tree, in an open space in front of the Giants' house, and the actors prepare for the play. But the Giants' servants, symbols of tastelessness and philistinism, do not want a poetic play. They want entertainment, not high art, but although Cotrone tries to persuade the actors to go along with them, Ilse refuses. She attacks the audience for their ignorance, and in their rage the Giants tear her to pieces behind the curtain on the stage.*

This missing final scene is the most crucial point about *The Mountain Giants* for me, and is weighted with responsibility for myself as interpreter. Imagine a vast play in which all the characters of Pirandello's theatre are found with all their words and gestures and, in a corner, the characters from *The Giants*, the actors with Ilse, the Count, all of them, in short, who cannot fulfil their story by a single word more because Pirandello never managed to write it. What a silence! They can only cry out their passion to a certain point and not beyond, because beyond that writer's final word there is nothing but imaginary movements and gestures in an action that has been denied sound. There are faces and mouths opened in a scream that will never be heard. Ilse's death, when she is killed by the Giants who cannot understand her, happens in total silence. In front of the lights of a bare ramp, lit with acetylene lamps that flicker blue and yellow, the funeral procession must become both heart-rending and tender at the same time, with the actors who have taken up the body of their dead sister showing in their faces, where the make-up has run, long dark streaks descending from their eyes, running down their cheeks. In the darkness of the empty stage only one lamp remains lit when all the others are put out, and it pulsates like a planet in the shadows without ever going out.

Giorgio Strehler, Production Notes for *The Mountain Giants* (1967)

Luigi Pirandello's prolific writing career, spanning the period from 1889, when he published his first collection of poems, to the year of his death, 1936, includes the publication of seven novels, six collections of verse, fourteen collections of short stories, sixteen one-act plays, seventeen full-length plays, and a great many theoretical and critical essays. His writing career is unusual in that he began as a poet and prose author and achieved considerable reputation in both these areas before turning to the theatre relatively late in his life. His movement into the theatre began in 1910 with his collaboration with Nino Martoglio, at the age of 43. He gradually increased his output of plays and in 1921, when *Six Characters in Search of an Author* had its premiere, he became established internationally as Italy's leading playwright. The success of his plays, both at home and abroad, led him to take the decision to set up his own theatre company, and in 1925 the Teatro d'Arte Company was established and Pirandello began a new phase of his career as writer-director.

One of the myths surrounding Pirandello's move into theatre, a genre for which he had not shown much enthusiasm in the early years of his life, is that he chose this alternative path when life at home, with his increasingly unstable wife, became unbearable; the fact that so many of his plays, particularly the ones prior to *Six Characters in Search of an Author*, have adultery and unhappy marriage as a central theme has added further fuel to this belief. But it would be more accurate to see Pirandello's move into writing for theatre as directly linked to his involvement with Sicilian dialect writing, for it was due to his collaboration with Sicilian actors and with Nino Martoglio that he was persuaded to go on writing and to extend his repertoire from the one-act format (based on earlier short stories) into the full-length play. His views on 'Sicilian-ness' are linked to his feelings about nationalism, and his essays on dialect writing show how he 'translated' the sense of belonging to a region into a sense of nationalism, a pride in being Italian and belonging to a great heritage of regional cultures unified in a new whole. With such views, it is easy to see how he came to collaborate with Mussolini and saw hope in the new fascist ideology of the 1920s, an idealistic interpretation of what was happening in Italy that had disintegrated into bitterness and self-imposed exile by the end of the decade.

Pirandello's central theme of betrayal and adulterous marriage was already present in his prose writing, long before his wife began to develop the obsessive jealousy which characterized her particular mental instability. The explanation for this almost obsessive interest stems also from Pirandello's Sicilian origins, where the code of honour ruled supreme and order in the family was expected to reflect the hierarchic order of society as a whole. And the theme of adultery provides an ideal mode for Pirandello's particular form of humour, defined in his *Essay on Humour (L'Umorismo*, 1908), which is both comic and ironic, amusing and profoundly tragic. Pirandello's plays are collected under the title of *Maschere nude (Naked Masks)*, and this is another deeply significant Pirandellian theme. The idea of the mask is both theatrical and existential. Pirandello suggests in the *Essay on Humour* that the mask is an inevitable feature of human existence:

Each man patches up his mask as best he can, the mask he wears in public, that is, but within each of us is another which often contradicts our external one. Nothing is true. Oh yes, the sea, a mountain, a rock, a blade of grass — these things are true. But man? always wearing a mask, unwillingly, unwittingly — a mask of what he, in all good faith, believes himself to be: handsome, honourable, elegant, generous, unsuccessful, etc. . . . He cannot ever stop posing and attitudinizing over the most trifling events and details — even with himself. And he invents so much and creates so many parts for himself which he needs to believe in and take seriously.

Pirandello's idea of the mask that human beings are compelled to wear as part of their existential predicament is powerfully metatheatrical. The characters he creates play games, delude one another (and themselves), and struggle to create structures that they believe have meaning. This vision of humanity was already well-developed in his prose writing before Pirandello began to find ways of theatricalizing it and transforming his philosophy into physical images.

Pirandello wrote a series of essays on the theatre and these, together with some of the prefaces to individual plays, provide an understanding of his writing that is fundamental. The passages in the following section, taken from some of his principle prose writings on theatre, are arranged in chronological order.

Spoken Action (1899)

What I mean by this is: dramatic dialogue. It would seem to be a suitable occasion to draw the reader's attention to this splendid definition which, alas, is not mine, since almost all contemporary dramatic output has its roots in narrative and derives its plot material from novels or short stories, rather than from drama, which is, inevitably, bad. Firstly, because a story in the narrative mode, generally speaking, cannot be adequately reduced and adapted to the needs of the stage, and secondly, because of the tyranny and, in my view, misunderstood rigorousness of modern techniques, a veritable Procrustean bed, which both restricts and diminishes that accumulation of material. It is of course true that even Shakespeare took the plots for some of his plays from Italian short stories, but which playwright ever transformed a story into action from start to finish better than he did, without ever sacrificing anything to the foolish demands of techniques that are only superficially disciplined?

Every descriptive or narrative prop should be abolished on stage. Can you recall Heinrich Heine's marvellous fantasy on Jaufré Rudel and Melisaund? 'Every night in the castle of Blaye one could hear a rustling, a scraping, a whispering: suddenly the figures in the tapestry began to move. The troubadour and his lady stirred their ghostly limbs from sleep, came down from the wall, moved round the room below.' Well, the dramatic poet must use the same miracle as that performed by the ray of moonlight in the ancient, uninhabited castle. For did not the greatest ancient Greek tragedians create that miracle once, Aeschylus in particular, breathing a powerful lyric soul into the grandiose figures in the magnificent tapestry of the Homeric epic? And those figures began to move and speak. Through the miracle of art, characters should step out from the written pages of the play, alive in their own right, just as the Lord of Blaye and the Countess of Tripoli stepped down from that ancient tapestry.

Now this miracle can only happen on one condition: that a language can be found which is in itself spoken action, the living word that moves, the expression of immediacy at one with action, the single phrase that must belong uniquely to a given character in a given situation: words, expressions, phrases that are not invented but are born when the author is fully at one with his creation so as to feel what it feels and to desire what it desires.

When we talk about *dramatic style*, a sharp, incisive, fast moving, passionate style is in our minds. But in talking about theatre, we need to extend the meaning of that word *style* or even to reinterpret the word altogether. For style, the intimate personality of the dramatist, should not emerge in the dialogue, in the language of the characters of the play, but should instead be revealed through the spirit of the story line, in the way this is shaped and drawn out and in the means used to develop it. If a dramatist has truly created characters, if he has put human beings on stage and not puppets, then each person will have a particular mode of expression, so that, in reading it, the play will seem to have been written by several people and not by a single author, and to be made up of individual characters within the action and not by a single author either.

Spoken Action (L'azione parlata)

Actors, Illustrators, and Translators (1908)

The most simple phenomenon that lies at the basis of the creation of every work of art is this: an image (that is, the one kind of immaterial yet living species that the artist conceives and develops with the creative activity of the spirit), an image that tends to become, as has already been said, the movement that brings it into being and makes it real externally, outside the artist. The creating process must emerge alive from the conception and through that conception alone, not through any contrived stages but freely, urged on by imagination itself which wants to liberate itself, to translate itself into reality and live. It is a question of creating a reality, as I have said, which will be the image become tangible. Together with the network of images structured within the artistic conception, there must also be a network of structured movements, put together through the same set of relationships, and tending to create an appearance which will not change the basic characteristics of the image, nor disturb in the slightest degree that spiritual harmony it lays claim to, but will bring it into the real world. All the features of the conception must therefore be found likewise in the execution.

Can this happen in dramatic art?

Unfortunately, there always has to be a third, unavoidable element that intrudes between the dramatic author and his creation in the material being of the performance: the actor.

As is well known, this is an unavoidable limitation for dramatic art. Just as the author has to merge with his character in order to make it live, to the point of feeling as it feels, desiring as it desires itself, so also to no lesser degree, if that can be accomplished, must the actor.

But even when one finds a great actor who can strip himself completely of his own individuality and enter into that of the character that he is playing, a total, full incarnation is often hindered by unavoidable facts: for example, by the actor's own appearance. This inconvenience can be improved slightly by the use of make-up. But we still have what is more an adaptation, a mask, and not a true incarnation.

And that same distasteful surprise that we feel when we read an illustrated book, and see the portrayal of the illustrator create a picture quite different to the one we had imagined of a person or a scene, is felt by a dramatic author when he sees his own play acted by actors in a theatre. No matter how much an actor tries to enter into the author's intentions, it will be hard for him to succeed in seeing as the author saw, in feeling as the author felt, and in transferring the character onto a stage as the author would have wished.

If the miracle referred to above could ever happen, that is, if we could ever read a novel and see the characters come alive before us out of the pages of that book and see them not as we ourselves had imagined them but as they had been conceived by the illustrator in the sketch that had affected us so distastefully, then we should surely feel a sense of outrage, like a nightmare, and we would rebel and shout: 'No, not like that, not like that at all.'

And yet how many times does some poor dramatic writer not shout 'No, not like that' in the same way, when he is attending rehearsals and writhing in agony, contempt, rage, and pain because he cannot see that the translation corresponds to material reality and that this must differ from the ideal conception and execution that had begun with him and belonged to him alone.

And yet, reminded by the author, the actor suffers too, in his own way, because the actor thinks and feels differently and perceives the author's vision and will as an outrage, and a nightmare. Because unless the actor wants the written words of the play to come from his mouth artificially, through a mouthpiece (and he cannot possibly want that to happen), then he has to reconstruct the character, that is, construct it in his own way himself. The image that has already been expressed must be taken back and restructured inside him so that it can become the movement which will carry it out and make it real on stage. For the actor, too, the process of making has to come straight out of the process of conception, alive, and only because of that can it have being, into movement suggested by the image itself as it lives and is active not only within him but becoming one with him, body and soul with him.

It will not be the same. It will be an approximate image that is more or less similar, but never the same. That given character on stage will repeat the same words of the written play, but he will never belong to the writer, because the actor has recreated him in himself, the character's expression belongs to him even though the words might not, the voice, body and gestures are all his.

And the same is true of the translator.

Illustrators, actors, and translators, if we consider the matter, all find themselves in the same position regarding aesthetic values.

All three are faced with a work of art that has already been set down, that is, has already been conceived of and effected by someone else, and the first must translate into another art form, the second must translate the material into action, the third into another language.

Actors, Illustrators, and Translators
(Attori, illustratori e traduttori)

Sicilian Theatre? (1909)

What are the reasons why a writer might be persuaded to write in dialect rather than in the standard language?

The act of creating, the activity of fantasizing which the writer has to use, is the same, regardless of whether he is using standard language or dialect. What is different is the means of communication, the patterns of speech. Now what are words taken like that in the abstract? They are symbols of things in ourselves, they are the larvae that our feelings must bring to life and that our willpower must move. And before feelings and will can intervene, the word is pure objectivity and knowledge. Now these words, this means of communication, this awareness, are universal, not universal in the abstract sense since there are no logical abstractions, but general representations. They are, for example, *house, road, horse, hill*, etc., in general, not that certain house, that certain road, that certain horse, that certain hill, with a determined way of existing and a determined and particular quality. Historical and ethnographical reasons, conditions of life, habits, customs, etc., either enlarge or limit the boundaries of our awareness of these objectivizations of things within us.

Now certainly a large number of words in a given dialect are more or less (give or take the phonetic changes) the same as those in standard language, but as concepts of things, not as a particular expression of them. An abstraction made from that particular feeling, even the concept of things, will not be intelligible wherever there is no knowledge of words as such. But there are a great many other words that can only be understood within the boundaries of a certain region, once the particular feelings and the special echoes that their sound arouses in us are taken into account, when they are considered.

Now why should a writer choose to make sure of such a restricted means of communication when the creative activity that he must make use of will be the same? For a variety of reasons, which limit dialect production as knowledge because they are indeed reasons of knowledge, of words, or of things represented. Either the poet does not have the knowledge of the widest means of communication, standard language, or else he does but feels that he cannot use it with the same liveliness, with that precisely suited spontaneity that is a principal, unavoidable condition of art; or else the nature of his feelings and images is so deeply rooted in the earth whose voice he seeks to be, that any other means of communication would seem unsuitable or incoherent except dialect; or else what he wants to represent is so local that it could not be expressed beyond the limits of a knowledge of the thing itself.

A dialect literature, in other words, is made to remain within the boundaries of dialect. If it goes beyond them, it can only be enjoyed by those who have some knowledge of that particular dialect and of its particular uses and customs, or a word or of a particular life expressed by that dialect.

Now outside the island, what does anyone know about Sicily? People have a very limited knowledge of a few characteristics, violent ones that have become well-known (fashionable).

The dramatic character of Sicily is fixed by now, typified in the terrible, marvellous bestiality of Giovanni Grasso.

Lacking any other awareness of Sicilian life in all its variety and diversity, clearly that expression of Sicilianness becomes almost meaningless. We are not talking therefore about the tastes and tendencies of the public, we are talking simply about knowledge.

A dialect theatre that represented the varied, diverse life of Sicily could only be enjoyed and greeted with enthusiasm in Sicily. Outside Sicily the only success it could have would be through those manifestations that are well known, that have now become typical. That is, Mr. Grasso and Mme. Aguglia can be successful because they don't even have to speak to be applauded; all that's needed is mime.

To sum up: do we want to create a truly Sicilian dialect theatre or do we want to manufacture a Sicily for export via Mr. Grasso and Mme. Aguglia.

That splendid poet and dramatist Nino Martoglio tried the former quite seriously and neither could nor did have any success outside Sicily, not on account of the tastes and tendencies of the public, I repeat, but because of the ignorance in which the public still remains regarding Sicily, regarding that basic first stage of any artistic creation, the cognitive material. Art is creation, it is not learning, but art is not created *ex nihilo*, it needs knowledge. It needs, that is, for the thing to first be known in the abstract and in the word which is its symbol and general representation, in order to be understood and to be enjoyed in all its individuality for the subjectivizing of the objectivity in which art consists.

Martoglio's attempt failed. Mr. Grasso and Mme. Aguglia in contrast are successful, but I do not believe that Sicily has very much cause to rejoice.

Sicilian Theatre? (Teatro Siciliano?)

Theatre and Literature (1918)

Writing a good play, a comic play or a serious one, does not mean creating characters who speak in a literary language, a language that exists only on the page and not in true speech. This kind of writing is elaborate. Characters should speak according to their own personalities, the conditions in which they find themselves, according to the action of the play. And this certainly does not mean that the result will be an everyday, non-literary language. Because what does 'non-literary' mean to the writer of a work? Language cannot ever be *everyday*, because it will belong to a given character in a given scene, and will be an intrinsic part of that character's passions and games. And if all the characters speak in their own special way and not in the vulgar carelessness of an imprecise language that only denotes the inadequacy of the writer who could not find suitable words because he does not know how to write, then the play will be well-written, and a well-written play, particularly if well-shaped and well-acted, will be a literary work in just the same way as a good novel is, or a good story or a good lyric.

Now it should be borne in mind that art in any of its forms (by which I mean the art of literature, of which drama is only one of its many forms) is not imitation or reproduction, it is *creation*. There is the question of whether and how language should be spoken, the immense difficulty of finding a language that is actually spoken throughout the Italian nation, and the linked question of the lack of a truly national Italian way of life that can provide material and character for an Italian theatre, as though the nature and task of art were the reproduction of that life which anyone can perceive from external factors, and there is the question of all the other distressing trivialities and empty superstitions of so-called technique that ought to reflect action as we see it happen before our eyes in everyday reality (at least in theory, because it is impossible in practice): all of this is a torture filled with the voluntary torments of an absurd system and an abhorrent poetics which is fortunately totally out of date but which, I must repeat, still holds the loyalty of the distinguished dramatic writers.

Theatre and Literature (Teatro e letteratura)

Preface to 'Six Characters in Search of an Author' (1925)

I wanted to present six characters seeking an author. Their play does not manage to get presented — precisely because the author whom they seek is missing. Instead what is presented is the comedy of their vain attempt with all that it contains of tragedy by virtue of the fact that the six characters have been rejected.

But can one present a character while rejecting him? Obviously, to present him one needs, on the contrary, to receive him into one's fantasy before one can express him. And I have actually accepted and realized the six characters: I have, however, accepted and realized them as rejected: in search of *another* author.

What have I rejected in them? Not themselves, obviously, but their drama, which doubtless is what interests them above all but which did not interest me — for the reasons already indicated.

And what, for a character, *is* his drama?

Every creature of fantasy and art, in order to exist, must have his drama, that is, a drama in which he may be a character and for which he is a character. This drama is the character's *raison d'être*, his vital function, necessary for his existence.

The birth of a creature of human fantasy, a birth which is a step across the threshold between nothing and eternity, can also happen suddenly, occasioned by some necessity. An imagined drama needs a character who does or says a certain necessary thing; accordingly this character is born and is precisely what he had to be. In this way Madame Pace is born among the six characters and seems a miracle, even a trick, realistically portrayed on the stage. She is no trick. The birth is real. The new character is alive not because she was alive already but because she is now happily born as is required by the fact of her being a character — she is obliged to be as she is. There is a break here, a sudden change in the level of reality of the scene, because a character can be born in this way only in the poet's fancy and not on the boards of a stage. Without any one's noticing it, I have all of a sudden changed the scene: I have gathered it up again into my own fantasy without removing it from the spectator's eyes. That is, I have shown them, instead of the stage, my own fantasy in the act of creating — my own fantasy in the form of this same stage. The sudden and uncontrollable changing of a visual phenomenon from one level of reality to another is a miracle comparable to that of the saint who sets his own statue in motion: it is neither wood nor stone at such a moment. But the miracle is not arbitrary. The stage — a stage which accepts the fantastic reality of the six characters — is no fixed, immutable fact. Nothing in this play exists as given and preconceived. Everything is in the making, is in motion, is a sudden experiment: even the place in which this unformed life, reaching after its own form, changes and changes again, contrives to shift position organically. The level of reality changes. When I had the idea of bringing Madame Pace to birth right there on the stage, I felt I could do it and I did it. Had I noticed that this birth was unhinging and silently, unnoticed, in a second, giving another shape, another reality to my scene, I certainly wouldn't have brought it about. I would have been afraid of the apparent lack of logic. And I would have committed an unfortunate attack on the beauty of my work. The fervour of my mind saved me from doing so. For, despite appearances, with their specious logic, this fantastic birth is sustained by a real necessity in mysterious, organic relation with the whole life of the work.

Preface to *Six Characters in Search of an Author*,
translated by Eric Bentley

Will the Talkies Do Away with Theatre? (1929)

Anyone who has heard me talk about the experiences of my many travels will know the admiration with which I have talked about America and the great liking I have for Americans.

What interests me above all else about America is the birth of new forms of life. Life, pressured by natural and social needs, looks for and finds these new forms, and to see them being born is an incomparable pleasure to the soul.

In Europe the dead go on making life, crushing the life of the living with the weight of history, tradition and custom. The consistency of old forms obstructs, hinders, cuts off any vital movement.

In America life belongs to the living.

Except that life, though on the one hand it needs perpetual movement, has nevertheless a need to consist in some form or other. These two needs which are opposed to one another do not allow life to have either perpetual movement or perpetual consistency. Consider that if life were to move forever, it would never be consistent, whilst if it were always consistent, it would never move.

Life in Europe suffers from too much consistency in its old forms, and perhaps in America life suffers from too much movement without any lasting, consistent forms.

So that in response to an American gentleman who boasted to me that 'We have no past, we are completely future-oriented!' I was able immediately to say, 'I see, dear sir, that you are in a great hurry to make yourselves a past'.

Forms, whilst they remain alive, that is, while vital movement remains within them, are a conquest of the soul. To destroy them in that living state for the pleasure of replacing them with other new forms is a crime, it is the subjugation of an expression of the soul. Certain original, almost natural forms through which the soul expresses itself cannot be subjugated, because life itself virtually expresses itself through these forms; therefore they cannot grow old and be replaced without murdering life in one of its natural expressions.

And one such form is the theatre.

My friend Evreinoff, author of a play which the Americans too have greatly appreciated, reaches the point of saying in one of his books that all the world is theatre and that not only do all human beings act out the role they have assigned to themselves in life, but that all animals act out roles too, as do plants, in short, as does all of nature.

Perhaps this is going a little too far. But that theatre, before becoming a traditional literary form was a natural expression of life, is completely and utterly undeniable.

And yet, in these days of great universal infatuation for the talking film, I have heard a certain heresy being passed around: that the talkie will do away with theatre, that in two or three years' time there will be no more theatre, that all theatres and music halls will be closed down because everything will be cinema, talking film or musical film.

Meanwhile, the theatre, both the classical and the music hall, can stay calm and certain that it will not be abolished, for one simple reason: it is not trying to become cinema, but the cinema which is trying to become theatre, and the greatest success it can aspire to, putting itself even further along the road towards becoming theatre, is to become a photographic, mechanical reproduction of theatre, one which is more or less good and which, like all copies, simply arouses desires for the original.

The fundamental mistake of the cinema was to set off from the outset on the wrong road, on an unsuitable road, the road of literature (prose or drama). Along that road the cinema found itself inevitably in a double bind, that is:

(1) in the impossibility of replacing words;
(2) in the impossibility of doing without words.

And with this double defect:

(1) an intrinsic defect, that of not being able to find its own free expression through the word (both expressed and implied);
(2) a defect in literature which, when reduced to a single viewpoint, inevitably sees all its spiritual values diminish, which can only be fully expressed in the most complex medium of expression available, the one which properly belongs to it, that is through words.

Now giving words mechanically to the cinema does not help the fundamental error, because instead of curing the sickness, it aggravates it, pushing cinema even more firmly down into literature. When the word is mechanically imposed onto film, cinema begins inexorably to destroy itself in order to become a mechanical, photographic copy of theatre, because cinema is the silent expression of images and the language of appearances.

So long as it kept quiet, so long as it was a silent expression of images understandable to all with a few brief written notes that could easily be translated into a range of languages, then the cinema was a sizeable rival or threat to the theatre, especially in recent times, because of its vast international distribution network and the taste it had succeeded in creating in the general public for silent performances. There were various signs that indicated how far the theatre was becoming concerned by the rivalry of the cinema: certain directorial abuses that tried to make theatre become a visual spectacle above all, or as much as possible, some imitation of cinematic techniques that occasional directors used, such as gradually darkening a stage and letting another emerge from the blackout, accompanied by music; the choice of a new repertoire of plays, a lighter, less consistent one, that could be easily manipulated so as to obtain the special effects of sudden changes and other devices specially laid on for visual impact. The great danger for theatre lay precisely in this attempt to resemble the cinema. And now, in contrast, the cinema is trying to become theatre. And so theatre has nothing more to fear. If I cannot see anything in the cinema except a poor reproduction of theatre, and if I have to listen to photographic images of actors speaking in strange voices through a mechanically operated machine, then I prefer to go to the theatre, where at least there are real actors speaking with real voices. A talking film may aspire to replace theatre altogether, but can only obtain the effect of making me regret that I do not have real, living actors before me playing tragedy or comedy and only have their mechanical, photographic reproductions.

'Will the Talkies Do Away with Theatre?'
('Se il film parlante abolirà il teatro?'),
Corriere della Sera, 16 June 1929

Address to the Volta Conference on Dramatic Theatre (1934)

The theatre cannot die. It is a form of life itself and we are all actors in it. If theatres were abandoned and left to rot, then theatre would continue in life, it could not be suppressed, and the very nature of things would always be spectacle. It is therefore quite absurd to talk about the death of the theatre at a time like this, so full of contrasts and therefore so rich in dramatic material, in such a ferment of passions and vertiginous events that change the face of whole nations, a vortex of incident and unstable situations where there is a continual need to emphasize some kind of new certainty in the midst of this tempestuous whirlpool of doubts.

It is true that life can either be lived or written about and that when it is being lived it is very difficult to put oneself in the right conditions for art, since one is right in the middle of all the action and the passion. Art requires one to start with the moment and go beyond it in order to consider that moment and to give it a universal meaning and an eternal value. What this means, of course, is that the drama of our lives will not be so much the theatre of today but will be the theatre of tomorrow. Art can anticipate life, can predict it, but to invalidate the life of today and to categorize it under *specie aeternitatis* is both rare and difficult today, though it will be easier tomorrow. Of course everything can be material for art and the artist reflects the life of his time, nor indeed could he do otherwise, since he is himself a product of a civilization and of the moral life of his own time. However, to do it deliberately, that is, with the intention of making it a practical, voluntary act of the moment, even though this may be for the best of ends if extraneous to art, is to make politics, not art. Of course, this is not to say that at certain moments in the life of a nation, art should not take on this role, as has happened many times, and become the tool of a noble civil or political act, that is, to diminish its own quality as art in order to remain an historical document, if not an artistic monument to the history of a nation's civilization. But at times this is not desirable or necessary or pertinent, and beyond any interested passion, art needs to be considered in terms of how its nature alone can assist fictions and inventions. Real, true documents can be of infinitely more value, together with facts, persuasive, eloquent testimonies through which art, by sacrificing and annihilating itself, would come to serve as an inadequate tool, since the mystery of every artistic birth is the same mystery as any natural birth and not a thing that can be made, just something that has to come to life naturally. Nor should it come to life through an author's whim, freely and outside all laws, as those who do not understand often falsely suppose, but should adhere to its own unalterable vital laws, in such a way that it is free from any taint of expediency because it wills itself to be and has no other aim than those pure ones within itself. If such is not the case, then it will no longer be a work of art and is therefore to be condemned, not only in the name of all things to which wrong has been done, but above all in the name of art itself.

In other times people were drawn to performances on the occasion of major feasts and great religious festivals. Now that no longer happens, and people go on a daily basis, drawn by habit that has become a need, which is a sign of a developing civilization. It does still happen that in the summer months or in spring people are drawn to extraordinary

89

performances in the open air, in ancient amphitheatres, for annual or biennial celebrations in certain cities, in piazzas or other designated places. But magnificent though these may be, they do not solve the problem of the theatre and with time every nation that seeks to be considered civilized has had to deal with a problem of civilization: closed theatres every evening. I leave it to you to decide whether the so-called theatre of the masses can solve this problem, or whether this concept does not derive from the opposite viewpoint — that is, for celebratory performances and grandiose one-off shows, like the athletics which draw such huge crowds. Yes, there is indeed a vast public, but all these performances are extraordinary and cannot, nor could ever, be mounted on a daily basis.

So far only the cinema has succeeded in satisfying this daily hunger for performances that is now so widespread. If we want the prose theatre to solve it, especially in the conditions in which it now finds itself *vis-à-vis* the cinema, then we must consider whether the time has not come to take the steps taken by some other countries and to limit evening showings of films to one night and at a fixed time. In this way the prose theatre would not so much be placed in the position of having an advantage, but would at least be competing on equal terms. The public would have to choose between types of performances, and the cinema would not have the advantage of being able to reproduce mechanically the same show, since until the cinema can find its own artistic expression, as everyone hopes it will, multiple showings are detrimental to the theatre. But we should also plan to build new theatres, just as new stadiums are being built for sporting events, since in the theatre we are still breathing the musty air of old places that are no longer suited to modern needs, not only the needs of art but also, and principally, the needs of custom and economics.

In all its manifestations, new life is fleeing from the old categories, both those of class and those of acquired privilege, and so the theatres which were built in times when those distinctions were keenly felt now give the impression of being anachronistic places from which we almost instinctively seek to distance ourselves.

It is to be hoped that out of the proposals and discussions held at this conference the most efficacious and practical way of attracting people back to the theatre will be in the building of new playing spaces, and perhaps in this way the question of the hoped-for mass theatre will also be solved in spirit. What is needed are purpose-built halls, capable of holding enough people to more than cover the costs of performances whilst keeping the prices level with those of the cinema, and with seating arranged in such a way that there are no other visible distinctions than the obvious one of greater or lesser distance from the stage: stages with new equipment, with all the technical apparatus needed to transform every performance into a spectacle, more suited and no less attractive than those to which the cinema has now accustomed people.

Stage designers have a huge open field here for their ideas and plans. And it is to be hoped that the question which has been debated for so long will be finally resolved, that is, whether the theatre is there to offer a performance in which the play — the writer's creation — is only one of the many elements controlled by the director, together with the sets, the lighting, the acting; or whether, on the contrary, all these elements, together with the unifying work of the director responsible for the performance, alone should not be put to the task of giving life to the play so that it can be understood by everyone, for without it nobody would have any reason to be there, night after night. By giving life, I mean the life that is inviolable, because it is coherent in every way, that the work of art claims for itself, and therefore it is not up to the director to alter it nor to manipulate it in any way.

The play is what remains even though it exists in time in the fleeting performances given in theatres. And amongst all the types of performance that can enter into the life of a nation for a time, the theatre is the one which contains and mirrors most intimately all moral values; the theatre is what remains. Giving voice to feelings and thoughts which are all too obvious in the lively play of the passions represented and that, through the very nature of this art form, need to be put in clear, precise terms, the theatre presents human actions as they truly are for honest public judgement, in all their eternal, clear reality created by the mind of the writer as an example and a warning to the confusion of daily life. That free, human justice effectively reawakens the consciousness of the judges themselves and reminds them of a higher, more demanding moral life. Every period of human history has handed down its theatre to us, living through different nations, and that theatre has always been a sign of a great moment in the life of those nations. It is a sacred, monumental heritage and one which all states, both great and small, have felt the need to accommodate with specific places of performance. Nor is it a museum of motionless statues, but a place in which the most worthy plays can continue forever to come to life, whilst new works that just happen to have been created can live outside all those adverse and precarious conditions of the present.

Address to the Volta Conference on Dramatic Theatre
(Discorso al Congresso 'Volta' sul teatro drammatico)

a: Primary Sources

The standard Italian edition of Luigi Pirandello's works is *Opere di Luigi Pirandello* (Milan: Mondadori), consisting of *Novelle per un anno* (two vols., 1956-57; new enlarged ed., 1969); *Tutti i romanzi* (1957, in two vols., 1973); *Maschere nude* (two vols., 1958); and *Saggi, poesie, scritti varii* (1973). By no means all of Pirandello's works have been translated into English, and in many cases English translations are long out of print.

Plays

The first, hopefully complete English translation of the *Collected Plays* of Pirandello began publication in 1987 (London: John Calder), and is in progress. *Three Plays* (London: Methuen, 1985) assembles *The Rules of the Game*, *Six Characters in Search of an Author*, and *Henry IV* in an inexpensive collection. Details of first Italian publication and of all English translations of individual plays are given under their titles in Section 1.

Short Stories
The following are selections, not complete editions:

Luigi Pirandello, *Short Stories*, trans. Lilly Duplaix (New York: Simon and Schuster, 1959).
Luigi Pirandello, *Short Stories*, trans. Frederick May (London: Oxford University Press, 1965).
Luigi Pirandello, *Tales of Madness*, trans. Giovanni Bussino (Boston: Dante University Press, 1984).
Luigi Pirandello, *Tales of Suicide*, trans. Giovanni Bussino (Boston: Dante University Press, 1988).

Novels

The Late Mattia Pascal (Il fu Mattia Pascal), trans. A. Livingston (London: Dent; New York: Dutton 1923).
The Late Mattia Pascal, trans. Nicoletta Simborowski, (London: Dedalus, 1987).

The Outcast (L'esclusa), trans. Leo Ongley (London: Dent; New York: Dutton, 1925).

Shoot (Si gira), trans. C. K. Scott-Moncrieff (London: Chatto and Windus; New York: Dutton, 1926).

The Old and the Young (I vecchi e i giovani), in two vols. (London: Chatto and Windus; New York: Dutton, 1928).

One, None and a Hundred Thousand (Uno, nessuno e centomila), trans. Samuel Putnam (New York: Dutton, 1933).

A Character in Distress (La tragedia di un personaggio), trans. Michele Pettina (London: Duckworth; New York: Dutton, 1938-39).

b: Secondary Sources

Susan Bassnett-McGuire, *Luigi Pirandello* (London: Macmillan, 1983).

Eric Bentley, *Naked Masks* (New York: Dutton, 1952).

Eric Bentley, *The Pirandello Commentaries* (Evanston, Illinois: Northwestern University Press, 1986).

Tom Bishop, *Pirandello and the French Theatre* (New York: New York University Press, 1960).

Oscar Budel, *Pirandello* (London: Bowes and Bowes, 1966).

Glauco Cambon, ed., *Pirandello: a Collection of Critical Essays* (Englewood Cliffs, N.J.: Prentice-Hall, 1967).

Martin Esslin, *Reflections* (Garden City, N.Y.: Doubleday, 1969).

Gaspare Giudice, *Pirandello: a Biography* (London: Oxford University Press, 1975).

F. L. Lucas, *The Drama of Chekhov, Synge, Yeats, and Pirandello* (London: Cassell, 1965).

Landor McClintock, *The Age of Pirandello* (Bloomington: Indiana University Press, 1951).

Jorn Moestrup, *The Structural Pattern of Pirandello's Work* (Odense: Odense University Press, 1972).

Roger Oliver, *Dreams of Passion* (New York: New York University Press, 1979).

Anne Paolucci, *Pirandello's Theatre* (Edwardsville: Southern Illinois University Press, 1974).

Olga Ragusa, *Pirandello: an Approach to His Theatre* (Edinburgh: Edinburgh University Press, 1980).

Richard Sogliuzzo, *Luigi Pirandello, Director: the Playwright in the Theatre* (Metuchen, N.J.: Scarecrow Press, 1982).

Doug Thompson, *An Introduction to Pirandello's Sei personnaggi in cerca d'autore* (Hull: University of Hull, 1985).

Since 1981 *The Yearbook of the British Pirandello Society* has been published annually. The fiftieth anniversary of Pirandello's death in 1987 also prompted several important publications, all of which are, however, only available in Italian:

Alessandro D'Amico and Alessandro Tinterri, *Pirandello capocomico* (Palermo: Sellerio Editore, 1988). [Contains a detailed account of the years of Pirandello's directorship of the Teatro d'Arte company in Rome, 1925-28, with many previously unpublished photographs and set designs.]

Michele Cometa, *Il teatro di Pirandello in Germania* (Palermo: Edizioni Novecento, 1986). [A study of Pirandello's relationship with the German theatre, including accounts of productions of his plays in German, with many previously unpublished photographs and set designs.]

Guido Lopez, *Caro Pirandello* . . . (Cariplo, 1987, offprinted from the journal *Ca'De Sass*, No. 91, Sept. 1985). [Previously unpublished correspondence between Pirandello and Sabatino Lopez, tracing Pirandello's movement towards the theatre from 1910 to 1930, with some unique photographs.]